THE
UNNAMEABLE
OBJECT

THE BOOK OF THE UNNAMEABLE OBJECT AS
DELIVERED BY THE PARTY OF MILD PROGRESS
WITHIN THE LIMITS OF THE LAW UNTO THEIR
BASTARD SON: A BLOOM OF THE 21ST CENTURY.

or

'THE BLOOMS BURIED GROPE' MEETS 'THE
UNNAMEABLE OBJECT' FOR EXAMPLE

or

THE UNNAMEABLE OBJECT

or

MEMING THE GRIMOIRES

or

100 PRAGUE CANTOS

Printed by etc.

That corpse you planted last year in your garden,
Has it begun to sprout? Will it bloom this year?

T.S. Eliot, *The Waste Land*

Adrian Henri, *The Entry of Christ into Liverpool*

for Dave Williams

CONTENTS

ONE	10	THIRTY-ONE	95
TWO	13	THIRTY-TWO	99
THREE	16	THIRTY-THREE	103
FOUR	17	THIRTY-FOUR	106
FIVE	21	THIRTY-FIVE	111
SIX	22	THIRTY-SIX	113
SEVEN	24	THIRTY-SEVEN	115
EIGHT	26	THIRTY-EIGHT	118
NINE	27	THIRTY-NINE	122
TEN	29	FORTY	124
ELEVEN	32	FORTY-ONE	127
TWELVE	36	FORTY-TWO	131
THIRTEEN	39	FORTY-THREE	134
FOURTEEN	41	FORTY-FOUR	137
FIFTEEN	45	FORTY-FIVE	141
SIXTEEN	47	FORTY-SIX	143
SEVENTEEN	48	FORTY-SEVEN	146
EIGHTTEEN	50	FORTY-EIGHT	149
NINETEEN	53	FORTY-NINE	152
TWENTY	56	FIFTY	154
TWENTY-ONE	58	FIFTY-ONE	157
TWENTY-TWO	61	FIFTY-TWO	159
TWENTY-THREE	64	FIFTY-THREE	163
TWENTY-FOUR	69	FIFTY-FOUR	169
TWENTY-FIVE	72	FIFTY-FIVE	172
TWENTY-SIX	76	FIFTY-SIX	176
TWENTY-SEVEN	80	FIFTY-SEVEN	178
TWENTY-EIGHT	83	FIFTY-EIGHT	183
TWENTY-NINE	88	FIFTY-NINE	189
THIRTY	90	SIXTY	194

SIXTY-ONE	197	NINETY-ONE	281
SIXTY-TWO	200	NINETY-TWO	283
SIXTY-THREE	204	NINETY-THREE	286
SIXTY-FOUR	207	NINETY-FOUR	287
SIXTY-FIVE	210	NINETY-FIVE	289
SIXTY-SIX	212	NINETY-SIX	292
SIXTY-SEVEN	216	NINETY-SEVEN	294
SIXTY-EIGHT	219	NINETY-EIGHT	295
SIXTY-NINE	223	NINETY-NINE	296
SEVENTY	228	ONE HUNDRED	300
SEVENTY-ONE	232		
SEVENTY-TWO	235		
SEVENTY-THREE	237		
SEVENTY-FOUR	241		
SEVENTY-FIVE	244		
SEVENTY-SIX	246		
SEVENTY-SEVEN	250		
SEVENTY-EIGHT	253		
SEVENTY-EIGHT	257		
EIGHTY	259		
EIGHTY-ONE	261		
EIGHTY-TWO	262		
EIGHTY-THREE	265		
EIGHTY-FOUR	266		
EIGHTY-FIVE	268		
EIGHTY-SIX	270		
EIGHTY-SEVEN	273		
EIGHTY-EIGHT	275		
EIGHTY-NINE	277		
NINETY	279		

ONE

Don't ask where she's from, she won't tell you.
Don't ask what she does, she can't say.

"It's okay, it's okay," we collocate and brim.
No beginning.
No ending.
No day in the life but that it goes on and on and it never ends.

The gray scales romantic and Benson-curve contentious.

She am shuffling.
She am smiling.
Her quarters are a home, but she was eleven when cobalted and fined for her youthful treason as we rummaged the rune-action of a bi-Helened revolution.

Donald Duck skulls and the Pulp Fiction soundtrack on a punk's-not-death cheap fruit loop.

Context imaginerials and rotunda-sized heart returns.
Radost FX in eepac tractor vanerials. Lavatory image wishes with the grin tone of a teeth muscle.
Dramatised and memorised as a cod-hangover named 'Wewillpushyou' and through and through you do to this daydream of birthday cakes
and Samuel L. Jackson.

"They were doing it. Right there on the stage. You could see them!"
Rivers of beer, he told us.

"Buy me a drink and I will show you everything."

Mum's mummer, you got your freedom, and you got all the
Farley's risks you deserve.
Playtime snot-noses pinched from abroad wouldn't flinch at a
supper of ketchup and stale cornflakes after leg danglers off the
Buccaneer by a salty young Terminator, business-leathered.
Out in the peppery lexicons of Opatov,
and window washers.

Eyes split from the nude lash of panelák lovelies and our great
expectations.

"This is the place."

Do not swallow.

French TV toe-cutters fishing for clues in the stone rose
tinted poets of a third-handed book sellers atoning for their
Americanness.
Laying waste to the rat bastard clinging of dutiful aspiration
drones. Clipping dreams with shards of Frankovka.

"There sure are a lot o'writers here,"

"Yeah, and they's got the goods."

All of Holešovice cries, "I cry!" and writes it down for St.
Kerouac to bless in inaugural bad tendencies of good-tempered
redress.

Havel christened by municipal shirt-thumpers. Grand designs
occupying sentient barrels of foreign-ready Kafka blasters.
Old town, new town, Golden Lane, Nový Židovský Cemetery.
And the first reel delves river-damp beneath trembling bag-
dogs and ill-informed keepers of the faith.

Sun culture obfuscated by geriatric hemp players undertipping
by proxy.

Tone deaf Russian army coats. Braving the winter witches
and homophobic landladies rustling boys with cow hands
at Želivského bus station terminal. Unprepared for joy of a
tangible colour.

A twenty-four-hour banana ride and three years of existential
tuning forks in the road on the road.
Spitting distance from the bug bard's abode.

Cold to the touch money money. Able to be around.
Should have.

The acid lasted.

First game ball thrown by
Sean.
Canny California screenwriter comes up with a harpoon to kill
the bad guy, and no 'thinkers' please, we is in the entertainment
industry after all.

"A fucking harpoooooon, man!"

Eyes jacked. Himalayan sack shorts worn inside out for
longevity. A Globe-took book cook. Kitchen migraine groans
mistaken for the first throws of Uranian love.

"Think again, world! I ain't your average queer."

The seeds thumbed in like limp willies into a Babička Earth,
hell bent on stuffing all the dumplings in Bohemia with
neutered Langoliers.

The unnameable object proliferating contractual eventual
obliterations unfuneraled or burny.
Cobain still warm, Zappa still sober and Jagger insinuating
himself into the castle pockets of an unfiltered, ciggy-shaped,
nude philosopher King.

Invited into the Unpronounceable Symbol's pill-piled book
of charactery and bleeding out a God anecdote to follow my
Thargian splundig.

And this is how

'The Bloomsburied Grope' met the Unpronounceable Symbol:

TWO

Threshold Tendrils flaked at the list of the lachrymose, depth charged rightly but enemies getting off light and prosthetic inviolate literary catchapoles lapping at each other's colloquial bread storms since the first wave till the latest dry period incensed corroborated.

'Anti' matters.

The road less travelled is filled with clichés, and the TVs in this panelák are turned up to eleven.
They's just getting Dallas through the evening Iguanas.
J.R. shagging nine staffs in seventies room decor.
Grannies' glass cabinets the size of, as yet, uninvented Russian spacetwits.
Krtek egg cups, chintzy duck kitsches and proud-proud Spartakiády annuals.

Red winners. Tarot tweets.

Hole punch tram tickets clocking into work when your Dad was ovular.

Born to be reviled,
all who move here.
A chance to hate ourselves together.

Blake, Rimbaud, Ginsberg, Williams, Bukowski, Armand, Nash, Vichnar, Watson and Carrithers crane their heads round their gin and tonics to see what's all the fuss about.
Paris of the nineties in a Romani handbag.
The taste of Reeves and Mortimer still thick on our tongue.

'Halcyon days.'
How she despised that phrase.
Her mravenec long legs our carnage. Her astrological pretensions our upgrade
and free fall.
Albeit temporary and replenishing in as far as years are decades and days are jam,

and tea,

and oranges.

And Ludvík Vaculík was there and Levi was there and Ginsberg was there, and Tony Wilson was there, and 'happy communism book' lady was there, and Lois Lane, and infinite versions of 'you'
in a parallel paradise incomparable.

Sarcastic sex and your car crash mothers.

Hollywood writers struck. Baseball players struck. And my first prick words,

'We own Prague,'

stilled inna rotten diary page of an alcoholic rudeboy responsible for no one and nothing, pointless and unpricking.

Relentlessly unworthy.

Our solipsist god on the rocks of a distant shoreline smirks as we in our fame tuck bedroom corners into our friends' patience.

Covid 19 not even a glint in your rickety paternoster, goes round and round and round in a Blur as yet unaccounted for.

"You live in my village. The landlord of the Spread Eagle barred you before you even came there."
"Parochial shit hole anyway," Tony barfs, and takes a seat with his wife where Ginsberg sat and told Dave,

"You don't 'try' to write, you just write!"
Tony died twelve lines later. Alan thirteen previous. The hanging man over the bigger picture.
This parochial lad measuring the apocryphal.

Breathe.

THREE

The mansion of a revolutionary train pickled by a host of
wannabe homeless, delusional Anděls
singing 'Zombie' to a frightened shop window mannequin.

The last generation.

Uncontactable.
Free.

Saving empties for empties.

Sancho Panza's got a sidekick in the Derby wishes he'd kept his
latest thought to himself as he wipes the beer from his helter-
skelter waist coat and tout-scrounged leftovers.

'Legs' delivers and spits in derisory.
Deserved and doubting.
Privileged pout-spanner.
Gutless wind-dinner.

Cue attempt to punch a best friend in his third world-sized
head for having and not wanting, for sharing and unsharing.
Wishing the punch
had landed.
Mighta
woke me.

And the longer you stay the more we have to say forandagainst.
You don't 'try' to leave, you just leave.

FOUR

So the prelude to the Livorno canvases and their unequalled dismembership claims ungalleried the remnants of this Scouse nouse and his shyness
in the face of Alphas.

Only in drink could the Bloomsburied proper grope at dreamscope connections between eternal themes and current conditions.

There was no space between actions u priori, nor histories that did not rhyme,
and no plurabellas primadonnas we wouldn't sleep with
for a hunk of chléb and a turpentine jar full of milk and honey.

Vampure cliques, but one school.
Everybody cheating off everybody else's avatar and wondering how the Bart Simpsons could possibly teach so little in such an endless way.

And they revoked their folks and invited them too. And the parents tossed fireworks under the saloon tables to the delight of their children's Promethean outlaws.

Never stop unlearning. The post man's sack unveiled.

"He was stealing from you all this time."

"I borrowed," you argued, "to better," in the belief that a feeling always trumps a letter,
and the weirder the feeling the closer the suns.

Words hide everything 'cept the lightning flash of your love.

And I bet you a glass-eyed dollar, we ain't all of us actually
sifting for gold.
Gold never brought no one happiness, unless it was lubed up
and sent where those similar suns don't shine.

StillweSift.

And don't you dare be are you.
Can't you have not says they.
So lays the groundhogs for a storm-welshing gambler about to
milk the seasons dry of their Columbus spunk by no delivery of
youth's sugary toothed promise.

The dark horizons our night clubs.
The stultifying summer of '94.
A thin sweaty Raven-Raven at The Doors extinguished by
ice cool Staropramens fist after fist till the Bloomsburied are
Bloomspissed and the meat shop sells meat and the water shop
sells water and we ask directions to a party
one universe out of time.

The rain-soaked casey pissing into U Krále Jiřího, where the
overblown underage moon the opening and closing of carriages
in their first confounding
babywords.

"Ooconchetup preestup a nastup dvesheshe a zveeyaree.
Preeshti stanitse, starometskee namyestee."

That dim, smoked cavern.
A lightless nirvana.
A broadsheet cuddled and we're ordered to drink.
A Stuttgart wallflower predicts our clans, and tentative tendrils
now reach into the alcoves of murderous philosophy goons
multiplying by the plane load and careering off to unknown
democracies and overpriced Penguins.

"The ghost of Franz Kafka visits and speaks to me. I have
written many essays about him, for myself only, so you can see I
am not a phoney."

The legends sputtered.
Made up for themselves.
Popping paper and tablets on an old cinema balcony vowing
to marry large breasted women with relatable quarterlies
dedicated to sharing only the most obscure answers to the
Globe's macroscopic problems.
And slimy dancers who move like they fuck.

In Roxy barbiturates, framed frenzies.
And not a single camera between us.

There was no bloodlust, but the soporific abattoir-noir
mullmull of a journaling bunch of pro-adolescent schizos
wondering how to get from one párek to the next on a salary of
sub-Dickensian wit.

Billions saved in a matter of minutes.
That is the goal.
Twenty-six years on and even John Bruce Shoemaker never
donated enough ecstasy to summon a cogent t-shirt peace
stroke amuse bouche coup; let alone a cogito ergo boom.

And U Hynků, and Marquis de Sade, and The Derby, and The
Thirsty Dog so embedded in the preternatural ramifications of
our dance-dance that the roses J.B. proliferated can never be
counted,
until numbers are love
and writers can trash their dictionaries with blazin', scathin'
novy-speak.

The most beautiful creatures outside of every minority
sideswipe anti-hero.
Passing the baton in codes.
Till our livers are cornered into a sharp dark circle, and clowns
run the shabby planet cracking.

What difference a genius?
What difference a lover?
What difference an audience?
What difference fame?

What pretty colours. What a wonderful club. We will stay here forever.
Yes.
We will stay here forever. Like this. Just like this.
Unchanged.
With faith.

Huggably Unhinged.

FIVE

Faith in the ties that bind us,
and the lessons we Duchamp from fire to Freud, and how to
unravel our connections without anybody noticing.

Adept at staying unnoticed. Used knowingly and unknowingly
to one's advantage and betrayal in the light of the fact that
genius is cumbersome
and one prefers to travel light.

Spotty poet hoodlums of fat lady wrestler philanthropy cadging
fags from strangers and corpsing over matters Pee Wee Herman
would not blush at.

Scott and Jasper playing my hand before Prague had dealt its
dealers dealt.

Then again,
and for underagainst, they could have,
for all and sundry, been
darkerly melachoded than we forswearers forswore.

That layer of drank, which psychosexuals yer blues in the
wonderful world you make for yourself and praise/regret the
minute you atrophy.
They youngered in self-deprecate,
for want of a purposeful partner.

And Schopenhauer chuckled at my scooping up Chairman
Mao's little red book from a Swedish hitcher, and posting it to
future Mike wrapped in coollegiate mushrooms from magic
Madchester.

SIX

The MicroFestival funnelling
'The Universe and the Algorithms Greatest hits Volume 1.'

Recognising Louis from the pork-pied, tongue-fried hat,
Brechtian beard and sympatico aspect if you keep your two
metres, eat yer greens and read yer Joyce.
Approachable and stand-offish,
wordy and quiet,
deactivated but proactive.

Sensitive as cold steel Finnegans,
and warm as a comfort-spinster misses her autodidact.

Two thousand and eighteen years since Jesus Christ sat on a
splinter and was stuck for something blasphemous to shout
about.

Act one. Flood Scroll Flood posting meridian Venuše ve
Švehlovce.

Flaubert bitter at being first on the PMF bill. Yet to be dug up.

Jousting for the combination to his glass house and Joycean
anatomising, till all is revealed in his uncut Garden and
Gagarin's birds-eye view foreshadowing our Riegrák picnic of
instinct-melon.
A loping cinematic thread we pull, and the hangnail twitching
of remembrance folded.
And back to the occupied street he sequestered to ratartat my
Withnails, and lubricate the I.

"But this bee's a scary fish," she said, *"when you unfold it."*

But isn't that what we love about it? And isn't that why we care? I mean there's no point in writing if the scary ain't there.

SEVEN

Don't ask her where she's from, she won't tell you. Don't ask what she does, she can't say.
All three roads lead to her
and she
is
beautiful.

I know her, and am singularly, ambidextrously, multinationally grateful to be who I choose to be what we remember.

I am-was when you-and-I am holding on
to the belief
we did hope that we are what we wished we could be
when we really will.
And I am that now.
Because you are me.

"Winner Winner Chicken Dinner!"

Now, look up!

The artist's manifesto crumpled in the hands of a friend's friend's weed dealer.
A slowpoke in a telephone box sharing his partner's speed to his partner's chagrin. And the taxi driver swears blind there is no rave out here at the airport tonight.

I Scorsese an end scene for memorables and you? You look like a rear-view mirror phantom.

I will can would see you and.
I am when suchly.

I go go budget.
I lapped the gavel.
Yesyes.
Mmmmm,
speeeeeed

EIGHT

TAB SPOT!

A 'Tab Spot' is any place where we might stop to enjoy a cigarette.

NINE

United...

we lie to ourselves.
We prepare for nothing.
We know what we are doing.
We don't know what we are doing.
We must prepare to defend ourselves against ourselves.

The image we see of ourselves; the image we project, is an amalgam of our own devious fictions.
We defend this lie unconsciously.
We defend this lie online.
We invest our time in the virtual; in the recorded, and the remixed.

Hypnotised by the illusion of success we emulate the impossible us.
We argue points that never existed. We suspected never existed.
We make up answers in order to talk our way out of the ignorance of not knowing the meaning of the question.
We know our fictions.
We kill for our fictions.
We advertise our sickness. We buy ourselves back.
We spend our life preparing to buy ourselves back.

And you lie to me. I love it when you lie to me. It takes the pressure off me having to do it.
Tell me who I am. Tell me what I must do. You seem to know me better than I do.
You see everything.

We were floundering, grasping at things which we conjured in fits of rage and fear. Which we imagined we conjured. You are all history whilst I am limited to this goldfish memory.

I remember something about war and something about peace and I remember I liked her legs, her laughter, and her mother's marijuana.

"Siri, am I crazy?"

The answer quickly returns.

"Why you should take this 'Am I crazy?' quiz."

Sweet release in a form to fill with my own personal truths, to be analysed by an algorithm prepared for anything and everything.

Thank the Lord.

What is your favourite sport?
Do you talk to yourself?
What is your favourite music genre?
Do you hate certain things for no apparent reason?
Are you taking this quiz voluntarily?
You invite your friends over for a movie night. Which movie do you watch?
How many friends do you have?
How cool are dead animals?
The weekend is finally here! What are your plans?
What is your favourite colour, you crazy fucker?

TEN

The genius loci lying low.
The wall fall and Velveteen Revolt chewed in a gummy vortex of
Mitteleuropean stammer-jams.

Lou Reed and Frank Zappa cuddling the boiling corpuscles of
the excitables;
griming the memoires of the stuck.

Ginsberg still ventriloquising the howl out the mouths of Beef
Stew babes and poetry has no timeline. Ask Bob Dylan.

A man in the crowd passes us a lit joint and we smoke up
as Masters of War slowly becomes recognisable, and the
angelheaded children about us hold tight to their Blake-lights,
dealing with their anger
proto-hermetically.

From Dave's hilarious farts to my own Holy Joems.
Tarantula academy melding Zen with Lysergics.
– Coronary Bypass Mistakes Gymslip for Long Lost Sister –
The second time the pet store rang, I just gave the bitch up.

Robert is there in hullabaloo,
licking the saline solution right from under his overseas pupils.
Published all his phenomenools in one fine, boxulcuted poodle-
champ.
City Primeval. New York. Berlin. Prague. New York. Berlin.
Prague. New York. Berlin. Prague. New York. Berlin. Prague.
New York. Berlin. Prague. New York. Berlin. Prague...
His-city blues of the new new decades.

"It never ends. It goes on and on."

"Berlin's got too many artists now. Would have worked back then. Too many artists now."

But Prague beats a mystical beat
and the new new world synthetic forgives the time lapse, and
we pick up where we left off, except I been divided by three and
have started shaving my ball sack.

Outlining the Flood performance in fluorescent crayons and
Robert's expansive lens-tinders.
Catching the eye of Thor for Loki,
and stop motion films will be our bedroom ladyman-hummers
as we make every lucky number count.

Garcia pissed as a newt at war,
haemorrhaging vodka clusters about how phones are
destroying our natural God-given peripherals
like some Texas bred jungle cat's gonna jump us from a
Prosecco/Sorbet emporium abomination and chew us out.

"Ahhhhhh, you're a sucker,"
Louis sigh-says.
My love of television, love and 'I believe in you's.

Really should have placed him last on the bill.
When you write strangle vines and killer bees you need to dress
right. When you corrugate letters and lip the tight rope walkers
of attitude,
you very well must mean to mean.

A resistance experiment at Punctum colloquialising the
Žižkostel.
Saints redacted,
and not one free chlebíček amongst us.

Beer frugalities and bloody spectatorials from tale gating freaks
manifesting their MumDads and hussy criteria.
In prayer aroma for woody erections, we climb over each other
to listen because our lives depend on it.

And like Wolverine's midriff, and Harlequin's tree house, we
hurt when we are combed into knots
and we are nitrous and out of breath
and the ratpack gives us C.P.R.
and we never want to leave this bar;
not till the radiation sickness still pulsing since 'Threads'
transmogrifies into respect for our fellow man/boat/sorrow/
Godot.

In the dream I thrust my hand up in class and enthusiastically answer I don't know what question. I am tripping over my tongue to say it right. I breathe deep and focus and speak carefully... Zero. Zero is the answer. It's from nothing to nothing. Returning. It means nothing, and so this, all this, is the blank canvas, always, and the things we do and say are the paint brush." I wave my hand like that, like I am holding a brush and painting the air. The room seems impressed. We are united. In nothing.

ELEVEN

Most slid down the rabbit hole. Some remain.
Van Goghed in their garden, unweeded and pledged
to do the civil service proud and log into the library of
antanswers only when bleeding and necessary.

Unlike us unemployable bumpkins bilging down the tunnel,
every shelf and memo, advertising hope in a hopeless void;

a blasphemy is a canny way to expel a novel in one simple
expletive.

"More than waffle," Waffleto guarantees, with a confidence
no writer that I know has ever attempted to stuff down their
trousers.

And so it is faith we are propoundpounding with these taut,
ribald, mad gestures and acceptance that what qualifies as
readable is probably off the mark.
Whatever they think they know, only serves to jail our impulse,
and whoever we think 'they' are, we are condemned to be less
than convinced of ourselves.

Jacobites bloodstained. Republicans in jelly moulds. The
president all shady ass, out in the open, and none of us are
supposed to be here.

Thisiswhatyouwantthisiswhatyouget.
A great name.
You get a great name.
Need a great name.
Oh, the grandeur of delusions.
To make a name for oneself.

Youwantityougotit.
Wedon'twantit.
Widow attics.
Widower cellars.
Late night callers.
Back door men.
A cat in a corpuscle. An army of white cells. The cage has teeth.

Andy the bridge between Cimrman and Rosewah; the Saint dwelling close to the river on which Melpomene climaxed. Janus implicated in art as it is in heaven.

A stage is a stage for a stage,
an underrated algorithm crouching, poised and ready to rage.

Set against the backdrop of a foreseen revolution, and the second act drop curtain (muddled together in Christmas images from a central firehouse mansion) of a time when lunaTICS run for government positions
and lunaTOCS merrily vote 'em in.

She can't say what she does and she won't tell you where she is from.
But slowly slowly we begin to see what she's up to.

We sympathise. We invade the entertainment of the idea that we were put on this planet by no one for nothing and we occupy and we resign and we order our food online. Magic that shit out of nowhere.
And we empathise.

So we search for others like us. And until we have connected with them all, I mean every single one of them, we will recline in geriatric frustration whatever the cuisine.

She is the bomb. And the calmer.

Listen.

The Vyšehrad air tastes good and home isn't home without a plan. The problem with Zen is we want it again and again.

But the cemetery is creeping closer and who hasn't been jealous of those famous tombs at some point in their drying days hanging from a dishwasher's martyr's cross. Subtle Punks. Angry dishwashers.

"You a cook?"
"No, man, I'm a food alchemist. The Globe kitchen is my laboratory."

Cool American. Deleuzeorian. Guattarian. Swapped my thousand plateaus for Dan's Golden Bough because that's where Eliot done did get all his know-how.

Intimidated by the brain poops
and giant padres
and stroppy Nováks
and Calamity Janes
and snowballs dodged, thrown from the back, spied in my peripheries and some kind of superhuman nerd aversion.
I concede – Garcia was right.

From I.M. Foreman (a Scrap Merchant to 76, Totter's Lane, behindacouch)
to 21 Lumírova,
and a poet bred by poets breeding poets, some of whom would no more call themselves poets as claim to know the difference between a tickly cough and a deadly virus.
And a penny for a pound that tear in the fabric of reality won't fix itself.
This is going to take some tongue twisting.

Memories wiped at the end of every draft. Not yet, not yet, not yet……

ZEN!

Cue, Jokerman – first inebriation...

"Now zen, now zen, now zen," in Scottish, German and French,
"What's goin' on ' ere?"

There's a message on the bench scratched in stale rohlík.
A familiar tune unrecognisable, in Vietnamese fisherman trousers, infinitely resizable.
And I kept on running.
I ran and I never looked back, said every man-Jack of us as I deteriorated into the sketch of a painting the proportions of which will bamboozle physicists for multilayered Oswalds.

TWELVE

Our presumed coherency of thought is mapped out
in the minds of dull-witted lunatics misread the moon's own
whispered mission statement to do to others as you would have
done to yourselves.
Founded.
Craters and craters of melancholy, aspect-tuned to the
frequency of a dead fish in an ISS captain's entrance exam.

"Person, woman, man, TV, camera."

In that order. Smudging the room till the bad spirits exit stage left.

'Liberal as fuck!' T-shirt reads.

Frankincense, cock-gold and meh.

"An event mass with a quantum probability of zero? I've been called worse."

The frankincense soothes. The cock-gold tempting and the end game? The result? Judgement day's catering team?

"Meh."

There will never be an end to the amount of humorous t-shirts we can make.
Rack 'em up, Jo, we've a long, long way to go.

THIS IS MY BOUNDARY

Our first attempt at a Nancy Bishop, with Maraschino cherries, salt and vinegar peanuts, and a plot to stage Plato's Symposium.

"Oh, man, sister! There's a promulgated Satanic goat taxidermy backdrop!"

Our pitch falling short by the length of a George Bush junior stretched out line of coke for a wannabe thespian wheezing at their suffering mother's apron string.
"We will call it, 'The Drinking Party',"
and put it in a jar.
And call it apolitical. And change our minds. And call it political.
Like all things political, with only the taxes to tell them apart.

I remember the light. The primary impress.
Then the dimming of the light as we described how we would stage the flashbacks and flash forwards and dream sequences, and all that distraction-from-a-weak-story-arc crap.
Nancy's brief, bright bulb sputtered and blacked. Dave and I revelling in the 'drama' business for exactly eight pints, twenty fags and one fatty sekaná.

"It ain't your room till you've been sick in it, bud'. Till it's seen you at your lowest and filmed you return to your minimal best."

Weapon grade atom Kaddish. Welts the size of horse flys' horses.

"The waiter's ain't out to make friends. S'what we like about 'em. Ain't even finished this one yet. Yes, I'll have another."

The big question is reborn and we redouble our defences in order to milk more visibly the tenets of nothingness.

Fuck the theatre!

"I mean don't get me wrong, I get along with God. We are both solipsists after all.
And yaahhhh, thought is as limited as God is limited.
And yaahhhh, neither is the wiser.

Our security depends on these limitations and from these limitations we create conflict, sooooo,
contribute or keep out."

"Well, I try to contribute," you say, "but 'they' won't let me in."

"Well, if you think that way, then I beg you keep out.
Put your house in order and don't wait for permission to contribute.
Our goal? To transcend thought.

To end knowledge.

To begin the story."

THIRTEEN

What these and those of them were.

With a certain measure of sugar we are
Free and Inevitable.

And there in the ballast of a crypto-carbuncle's contrary library
cures David the Vichnar;
a St. Nickelodeon with bars o' books for brain-curated chimney
strokes and keep the fire burning.
Equus Dominum, father of the P.O.D.
Pulped on Demand.
Pizza Orders Deliberate.
No time to waste.

Moulding the minds of Moravian munchkins, foreign carnies
and dutifully climbaboards.
Office musty.
Dusty a callback.

Masaryk and Beneš coddled Štefánik and Čapek to the
haunting-folk warblings of a petrified Jan Hus.
A romantic arboretum labelled freely by 'free presses'
perpetrated by the peoples I endeavour to promote, via
skywriting and tramping and mushrooming and reading
everything that peoples write.

"What is the power that moves an art 'scene'; moves an artist?"

"Someday I shall have finished learning, and then I will do
something."

"I will be the one to record the cruSCi-Fiction in words that those and these of them will be!"

"I know you will, baby. I know you will."

And the propulsion is a lava quagmire pouring down Sisyphus' mountain to a puddle at the toes of our dark blue stockings and ink-stained turn ups.
And listening to Morphine meant you were meant.
One step back and into the belly of a beastly bar steward coddling us like a table doused in the history of zelený-thinkers. They grow to the size of Georges Batailles, then publish his remarks in an effort to lose some weight. Conspiracy to shrink to the size of border collies and publish Vítězslav Nezval in an enthusiastic attempt to combobulate our cobblestoned diluvial.

But the question still remains,
'What move moves a movement?'

What moment raths a mome?
Will we look back and cheer at what these and those of them did?

Oh to be cruSCi-Fied between Gestas and Dismas the day before Christmas when you partake of throat fucking spine carp and earth apples zapped with MYANnaise, futuristically, six hours before realsies yuletide washes our very dark blue socks white and plays my favourite Christmas song.

And it's not only God who can make a tree; Jo makes 'em too.

FOURTEEN

The Guinea Pigs routed the bookshop at the christening.
The nail on the wall of the balloon poppers wriggling.
The acid unjoined from the past realigning.
Ludvík holding my head under the Baileys tap till I come up
shining like a 'found' penny psychologist.

Nostalgic for the present in retrospect. Barnes calling through
the intergalactic keyhole,

"I see an elephant in your pyjamas!"

And Ginsberg spat it out, and Vaculík spat it out, and it was
lost for some time, but I found it under the counter in the
bookstore; a boyish grin away from Ben's vegetarian chilli and
Sean's speedball-coveted closet.
There on the floor. A tiny, sticky ball. Could have easily been
lost in the dust and detritus of obfuscated holiday readers, but
throbbed into sight like a gay romance.

Our microdot.

Quantum theory born around 1900.
94 years later.
9+4 = 13
Death.
The unnamed arcana.
The unnameable object.
U.O.
And so linear time ceases to be.
And nonsense becomes poetry.

Inthistime.

We are skylarks on a mission into infinite states of movement,
and our thoughts are not houses
and our ideals belong nowhere
and our fleet feet tapping on stepping stones across this
infamous brook of fire.
And there's a lattice.
A gate full of locks and lovers and souvenir signifiers left where
we put them.
And leave them behind.
Other lovers.
Your James Dean life-size cardboard cutout cremated on
Janovského street.

Step round the dog-eared drunks cowering at the rear of
teachers' lounges and encompass nature with the sinewy
fingers of Egon Schiele and the cartoon tracings of Alphonse
non-locally.

There is only one way to hit the ball.
Choice is now out of the question.
We are in a state of non-confusion.
Be more Bjorg!

Miroslav Holub careens off Pierre de Lacenic and redeems
sexual tennises in Vyšehrad undergrounds.

Makes more sense.
Oh,
Diamond Day.
Oh,
Pizza Donna.
Král Majáles.
&
Fin neg ans Wake.

Ja ro mír baked. Free and Won.
Curly fries well into the next century.
The Literary Lavatory erection on the godhead thus far.
A massage stone in the Hubbard shoe.
A hex up a Crampus.

A soon to be crown of thorns in the side of the sadomasochism
between Fluxus and a giant Pooka.
Give us that ginger haired acorn hugger daily and I'll show you
the way home. His Diamond Day upon us all.
Unctuous.
Jaro', jako...
like... a two-tier promenade jutting out into newfound Luna
oceans and a fairground on the pier casting shadows on the
earth.
A strategy born of dead poets' ectoplasm moulded into a
birthday cake the shape of Neo-Disney's Public Enemy No.33.

Who will fight us clean? Who will doff the leather? Who in the
name of Centrála will untrope the bloodlines cross ten crown
L.P.s made lustful in crayon?

Saturday in an easy-listening kaftan. Petr Pane.
A Steinbeck jug of whisky addicted to chlébs' crusts and
improvisation's nervous pelvic thrusts; copulating in a hemp
haystack of prayers and offerings to the dark lord of mayhem
and typewriters.

Death to the charlatans!
Death to anything but bittersweet symphonics!
Death to all free angels.
Finn MacCool, come back! Get cultural!
Heaven's got nothing for the likes of you.
Ring them bells and let's have us a little confusion.
You stand up tall
and I'll pour on the cream.

And the Children of Lir teach themselves. Out of the pockets of
maudlin St Patrick.

"I am self-taught!"

If we do have an Andre Breton, a Louis Aragon and a
Gertrude Stein, they been sublimated in a scene fucked by
the transparent post-rub-structures of literary mummies and
daddies we left on the left bank of the nineties with a tram

ticket each and a comforting, "Don't worry, I know what I'm doing. We will look after each other. And if in doubt, don't ask a policeman. Prague knows where you are."

Where we quote unquote.

And together, all together,
Object Paradise bloods the Literary Lavatory,
and it rains stains on the shy.
Shine-shine Word Addicts and clement editorials shoehorned into a finite tome during low flying Multilingual Poetry Evenings stokes the lithe thighs of Medium 43 we call pleasurable Symposium in irony of a youth well spent.

Talking like an Alien, you pack me into my own suitcase, and now I can't take myself anywhere.

Rex-Patriots subli-mated, magisterial hallmarker rowboats
Overflowing with David Černý's well documented mistresses.
A Twisted Spoon found in your Celtic trouser press, and the Prognosis?
Open another club.

The time

is

ripe.

FIFTEEN

Stewed beef subtitles hurt my eyes
and Brandl's Tam Tam now tomb tomb.

Fan on full, and another corner turned in death-circus flourish
as Radost FX becomes home to the first edition.
Uncool Max putting his leg round the back of his comedy head.
Hopping on the spot till Willie kicks him shook to his toadstool.
Daydreams of boxed superheroes and twiddling twin Globes.

Ken and the painted American caves.
Soluble nudes and directions home.

The handsome troubadour keeping the kettle burning.
His rifle, his Manhattan Waffles and his stories twisting him
good.
Life-drawing words back to life. Naked insoluble.
These are real people we are talking about here. Real
confusions. Real surprises.
Call me surreal one more time and I'll gag you with well-read
bananas and tie gibbons in your hair.

Ken,
the private eye, understated and understating.
'Cept he's made up of a thousand platypuses. Each one
chomping at the steaming volcano bits spewed from his Titanic
imagination-gremlins.
He's neighbour to Faust,
and E.T. cleans his yard.
He makes everything easy look not very hard.

And the enclaves of his secret bedrooms and.

Technically, just waking up in the morning is an act of war.
We raise our pens and charge; charge for enfolding.

Not a soul sees their father. No father no soul.
Always close to discovering.
And what of our siblings' scribblings?

Mother, no mother, mother, no mother, born from the leg of a terraformed rock.
Their theoretical brains captured in the full ripened grain of accumulative aspiration drongos.
Well-meaning camomile clip-watching fembeds. All in an attempt to find the singular location of our hmmm hmmm home world.
Upstream.

No such thing as solidified solidarity.

Cue the music and opening titles after a drawn out, ten-part, preliminary show sequence.

Loading...

SIXTEEN

I was born unusually young
To a long lady.

"My friend was an extra in Casino Royale."

"Everybody was an extra in Casino Royale!"

And the polarities crossed, and the imagined cumulated in a house of monogamy.

The bent exoskeleton of past wishes gored and eaten by time's savage tastebudding marauders.
Guns and go-carts and species-red markers ricochet off Letná Park's scheduled guided tours like ancient friend-castanets.
Famous friends.
Water-tunnelling through the mansion I promised; the mansion Devo weaved.

Happy to be sad. Incapable of deception.
I love their viruses.
We poison each other.
Poetry-sceptical.

No, not you.

SEVENTEEN

"I spy with my mental eye..."

Did you know him when you touched him?
I didn't.
Do you know him now?
I think I feel.
Do they see?
I think we are one.
Do they see?
The eye does not see itself reading.

But the bullhorn of rain in the night of the calling gave each of us away like a father like a father like a father...

Like a

bullet-buried-wordword.

And she said..."It does not equate. Your desire to do what has never been done, and your reverence of celebrity."

The sharp bullet climbed up the polling station and all metal was cajoled off the peak by makeshift anti-cacti and orchid shamans we once thought rude for mocking amateurs their enthusiasm.

"And think of me," he said, in response to our repose.

"We shall not label that which is not. But think about me," he said again.
And we did.
And we labelled him.

But the psychical elements involved in choosing a path one might deem propitious are insurmountable.
Better to say 'fuck it' and let the bomb bring it all together in its own sweet bang bang.

EIGHTTEEN

And on the walls of his home hang
the vestiges of an impressive painterly past turned graphic
literati-illuminated
future-Lou.

The collage bionics of a family man's man.

Proud 'n' drunk to his drinkless steadilies.
Quiet and rogue and undefined.
Parades when deep in thought his circus-mind and alt thespian,
critic, director, starlet dinosaurs put there by God to test the
insane.
Hugh's muse explicated like teen-jewels surface-discovered
and altruistically offered as a gift of friendship and trust
virtuosities.

Claire bear there with green taught roots teached.
Welcoming butterflies in her smilesing breeze of Irish
alimentation cruises from living room to kitchen in an easy-to-
read trail mix of comrade ships.

No filibusters but Dolly Busters.
No Karma qualms but Dharma barms.
No busied quackeries but coddling Mummeries and Dadderies
in unveiled charmer bunches, savvy salad bowls and hombre
home mades.

Samira and Vít via Coleman, Waite and Smith undulate
the fallout peaktrough afterparty with Mad mild power
supplications for this scouser smokered.

An unloveable, clumsy object on the pavement excitable.

Child come trench warfare Martian gone bye-bye.
Samira and Vít waiting patiently.
Acrobatting high wire acts waiving white outs and pluralising.

"What do you make of this Tarot spread?"

Unannouncing myself dead in a Mandragora toilet cubicle
grave, gradualolligagging resurrection like a stringless Fraggle.

Samira procuring an Uber-familiar.
Spilling home to my enabler flat maters František Skála's
Dynamo fish cage.
The synapse bio-ethics of the withdrawal method and the
crunchy nut cornflakes of a writer's soul.

To not be shot at. To not be shot at.
The balm of
tonotbeshotat.

We are free people. Why cling to an unspoken promise?
The dictionary is a lie.
Show me her corpse.
Take off your suit first.
Now show me her corpse.

But I crept out of the corpse. And I deposited dust.
Like bible-droppings.
My equilibrium powered by proxy.
An artist is only as strong as his strongest critic.
And we all sat down.

The clans merrily being skewered by their own gay petards, in
the 'Okay' yard.

In cigarettes we trust,
in Musk we must,
and in trouble in all forms, and in Q Anon.

Welcome waves of mutilation scattered in Peaky Blinder hats

and braces. Guaranteed to make you bleed.
5-4-3-2-1... the cold hard stare of the morning melting into a flirtatious glance through the bottom line of a forty-five crown Kolčavka and a kick in the head.

Not just yet, so.

NINETEEN

The hundred metre reel of paper you listed everything on,
flapping at your boot heels as you trip to read next your mile
long grasp of the things most people dare not utter even to
themselves
let alone in polite society.

"Bless you. Bless you. And bless you. Consider yourselves
blessed."

Tyko has micro-managed the eager crowd with a culmination
of his finger bangs, dancing limbs,
Charleston nightmares,
big night out and makes you feel it, coooooool like,
like, like, like a Fallopian tube slif surfer nixing the candlestrop,
ovulating the demonstrate and pixelating the corporate.

The King of May ReturnReturns againagain to read aloud from
Shakin' Steven's Tempest.
Wearing a clown crown, eating a one hundred- and twenty-
thousand-dollar banana. We love him, and that dark 'in'
comedy.

We cold-reverse the Babylonian Hollywoodites and all the cock
lovers
and easy Tarologists are rubbing themselves up against their
favourite quotes till they can cradle their life-giving fluids in a
communal trophy cup of smugness.
And when we hear the poetry; really hear the poetry, we see
everything in its original black and white.
The way the universe sees it – not sees it.

But I see you.

In colour. A blue colour. Only one I'm good at.
Mum says I could be better at the other colours too if I just applied myself. She said that's what the teacher said and so she's saying it now.
How much easier it would be if we could just wear our mother's hand-me-downs instead of worrying about not being her.
She bought most of your clothes anyway.

And her life flashes before the audience's eyes and my sister's blood rushes to my head and I decide to accept it all. Everything they said.
James Dean did a weird job of acting old in Giant. Makes me uncomfortable.
The sky was blue when he died.
Dad will live forever. The barbecue's still hot.

"You could make toast on it in the morning!"

A p.c. storm in a houby.
Suckling daddy's artificial tit well into adulthood. Spectacle embarrassmente. Humankind finally outgrows religion.
Down with generation gaps. Up with gerontion.

Sue Suleman.

Comfort zoning laws approved by local nellies. "Wet blankets to be provided to all," sez King of May.
Cake force-fed to asymptomatics.
Neutral articles pickled in brine
Nakládaný correctness.

Him's diamond lyrics hid in the album cover squiggles. Finding proof in the non-existence of an interventionist God by taking considered notes on the different sizes of churches.
Feet squared.
Umbrage taken at the lone ranger's loving spoonful left behind on Tonto's saddle.
Medium 43 giving the bad guys a run for their money and propagating pleasure domes in place of inflammable-boob jobs.

She gets her pleasure in our leisure.
Nostromo underarms petting the pug.
"I can't breathe in this mask," it grunts. "I can't breathe."
And the pug is paranoid and laps frantic thirsty at the Bloomsburied Grope foot feet.
Spills the red, fiery hair aspects of our later works to be trod into the cracks of the crazy paving by a birthday gathering of teenage girls in Bobby sox and frank tops.

TWENTY

Wouldn't it be noice.

Beeple Crap whacking the lecturers,
keen astro wobbles and scratched Hancock L.P.s.
Tomáš Jetela Klooting collage porn gifs.
The art weather will be weather, and we are all sleeping bags full of jutting teenagers.

Refuse men snapping at unexplained installations left in the driveways of adult grown-ups.
There isn't a project unrambled by us seeksayers of ingratitude.
There is however one route untrodden.
The 'no' route.

Wouldn't it be loverly?

No more meetings. No more titles. No more event locations.

Klára Sedlo whacking professors' cold fusion equivalents of other gallery understatements nailing joy to a flying donut.
Landscape portraits of Seamonsters played live by the Wedding Present.
Merch sellers posing for the entrance application to Rock'n'Roll limbo.

"Nothing we can make can ever be big enough."
No more making. No more selling. No more grails.

Then in March the Lazy Fuckers – voices raised to ragged speeds. Beatles in sick memorium. Word perfect junkies tripping the late fantastic.
The dog-eared, cigar-hole-pages of novels tossed into the

Vltava.
Teaching the swans origami sex positions and mafia style double taps.
Wine-pissing gargoyles standing on the shoulders of cherubs.

"So let's just stay out tonight and over analyse everything.
How's that for a plan?"
"Maybe we will get there the back way.
I have faith in us."

And the new world waiter decides for Jo, "No, Mam! No! You will not have sugar with your coffee."
Jo does not capitulate. Not a capitulator. No.

Her paragraphs warm autumnal mists,
and everybody's happy.
Not the waiter. No.

TWENTY-ONE

"Any word which can be translated is a courtesan."

Don't ask where she's from, she cannot say. Don't ask her what she does. There is no translation for what she does.

"The thing in itself cannot be translated."

A true philosopher would never stoop so.
Hanging from the rafters.
Shifting at the worders' borders.
Robert taking timeless photos of the mannequins of prostitution our decades regurgitate.
Drooling, ambitious amateurs dangle on his black-black shirt tails and emulate his perfect semi-hair, his Demi-gougeish angel blonde and oxy acetylene story shorts.

Omnipresent documentalist behaving his way into the minds and hearts of clans of all nose breathers south of the arctic burp-melt.

Robert don't act no more.

But, oh boy, there's methodic arms in those sleeves! And those sleeves have been everywhere.
A more palpable history-synecdoche you will not find.
A more amiable gringo, clarity-savant, tectonic Bilbo, bon vivant, shape-shiftless, energy stalwart, lone-gang, you should be so lucky to 'like'.
A shoe on the other foot. A luxury pie of a different making. A friend of a made up blue.
A blue I get.

They don't build 'em like you no more.
Every night is Friday Night when you shuck the hands of
Robert's Bobness.
Free advice dressed in black because black is cool.
It really is.
Don't you forget it.

Don't put VHSs in the mouth of an alligator.

And as we conjure our joy bombs for Medium's Symposium
we calculate how much we can achieve by loving a neighbour
without physically being there.
Social distance based on faith, and faith based on nothing but
the truth.
You however are not make-believe.
My fantasy garden girls eye-catch wonderwalls; rubble in your
wake, tremble at your cookie cake, agonise over how anyone
can match the insoluble,
nude, almighty
you.

And Jo's breathing underwater-echoes of her future tumultuous
tunnels,
hair wet
with screams
and YouTube trollery, mindjob schooling,
Erica metempsychosing in rubber duck containalls,
leggings optional, beer-candles flickering like a mnemonic belt
buckle in a hadron collider.

Erika miming, seriously playfulness,
sculptor/media artist with a sticky bonbon soul pouring
childhood curiosity into a fundamentalists' existential vacuum
and squidging out the artistic,
metaphorical equivalent
of Samual Becket frosting a funeral cake.

Jo, doom scrolling to her heart's discontent.
Doom scrolling like a crazy person.
Spitting furiously quotations from idiot know-nothings; the

stage her set-up; the stage her home; the stage her kitchen-pirate,
Maltese sokolovna.
Louis leaping from seat to seat like a speed-thesis, to see it all fits, and close with a joke,
and in the future somebody laughs,
but in due consideration we sign yes it's okay to beginagain again;
yes again you may.

"Knock knock."
"Who's there?"
"Knock knock."
"WHO'S THERE?"
"Ding dong..."
"Oh for pity's sake! Not today thank you!"
"He's not answering. He's in there. I can see him through the fucking frosted glass. I think it's him. Knock knock."
"Fuck off!"
"Who's there!?"

TWENTY-TWO

In the nature,
for example,
Richard Makin's works "are what they are."

The Interior Ministry's works on the third hand, are
corroborations of various languages, and language's
dynamic dialects, spied familiar characters in obfuscated
circumstances, outside a caravan across the way from their
own, on the campsite Grande Meta-rie, sun-dried after a dip
in the pool, and coaxing long remembered flavours from their
hypermarche-adventure-fish.

She wanted to marry a fish.
She told her Dad she wanted to marry a fish.
A bigger small pond of gigantic miniatures.

As one teenage language touches another
in the twilight bushes blushing and hard and soft,
the skywriting now murmerates in epsilon.

"I wish my husband was ripped like that. I wish my wife was
funny like that. I wish my children were smart like those. I wish
my home was more like this."

And on one page David marinates the elder's blunt ineffectuals,
multiplying zero by corrupting lurid alphabets.

Homonym retrials batbat.
Hominymum legleg.
Hominymarmarm.

A mad, powerful nostalgia to Louis' work (on the fourth)

buries itself in the lipstick of prophesy and the Mulligan of
acceptance. Unacceptable.
Blows through his straw into his lemonade in defiance,
and an attempt to recapture his lostinspace childhood. Self-
effacing a flat white wall. Unfocused patois focused by default.
He arms himself with the impenetrable and demands you take
up the breadcrumb trail.
Jack Palance saying 'Pick up the gun,' in Shane.
George's 'burgin' drinking itself into existence.

And all the arrows and all the shields and all the shiny golden
horns
and all the king's manly men
couldn't protect us from Šárka and her ancient, naked
volleyball team in the snow.

And so we rebranded.

We are now 'The New Party of Moderate Progress within the
Bounds of the Law 2'.

Silent Sigh himself has the Prague police commissioner's
personal phone number.
And Shiva collaborate, and Bellamy collaborate,
and you read it and we'll paint it
and we'll dance about your local architecture
and provide fake tours for the world weary
and if we do have children, what's in it for us?

Pointing her gun at me, the Ivorywhitecop replies, "Evolution, baby! EVOLUTION!"

Dance dance.
Dance dance.
Reverse.

'Loud Noises' christening itself and ladling in two scoops of a
lager belt;
Justin, Daniel, Dan, Tim and 'I Am' salting the airwaves and
Tri-weekly music halls with Independent tunes post line-

concocted readymades.
In and out, in and out, in and out the bathroom, speed
tempering the waywards till forgiveless dawn offs the moorings.
Stuck in feverish excitement and happy dance, bumpbump to
the sound of our own clit clatter.
Peach Pit revelling Raveonettes, Black Angels, Tigerbones, Acid
Eaters, Oh Sees. Indie-surf-afro-punk-funk-Japanese-bop-beat,
and all the best music 'at the very moment' ever!

Then, with an egregious flippety flap, it was always going to be
nostalgia music, however quick off the mark we pinched it.

'Mixcloud and the Charge'.
Of course you remember us. Of course you do. You do!
I mean, you do.
Remember? I Mean.

The Zoo was dry.
The air was polluted with only pollution.
A heller was a heller and a lad was a lad's lad and so was a girl.
Communications' gospel, a post-it note on The Globe
bookstore wall.
The Kafka medium bees bullied by the terminator.

"Is this man your friend? Are you friends with this man? Would
you call him a friend? You should pick your friends more wisely.
This man is a bad man. This man is a very bad man,"

Kafka's champion shook
with his cold, and his coffee,
and rattling read rations returned to his seat at the safely
policed discount window.

You steal with soul. All the good men do.
You troll with soul. All the good poets do.
You Rock with Roll. All the good poets do.
You folk.
Good.

My school satchel kills fascists.

TWENTY-THREE

Prague, my love, I hate you so much today.

You touch your bronzed thigh as you read me your histories.
Your long, golden hair, braided and twinned.
Another 'you' somewhere within.
I dribble a little on your chin, and we start all over again.

Your tart orange heart lighting the blueblue graves and the
Čapeks and Dvořáks and Smetanas and Burians unfreeze;
sit cross-legged on the grass and listen along with me to the
magpies and pigeons and blue tits and kestrels,
wedding bells and you.

The happy parade of car horns irritating the cross-eyed
picnickers.
The thin summer dresses placating. Sitting here missing out on
any chance I may have with the ladies in waiting.

Quiet now.
The fire in our loins a cool, bathing sympathy-symphony rang
out in a campanologist's iPhone ringtone.

Prague, my love, you make me want to be another man,
as well as the one I am.
One of me could leave and not have to return, but he would
return,
and he'd dress better.

You cannot see through me. Your gaze is elsewhere always.
And how is it the others seem so independent? And how is it
you want for nothing and keep hold of us all? How is it you
want for nothing!? Where rests your gaze?

Why don't we care?

"Your Mum wants me to tell you how good you were."

Knock knock.
Knock knock.
Knock knock.
So frustrating that
I
can't
see
you.
The words slowdive the moreyoudrink. Colder. But not deep.

Lawrence Wells calls down from the balcony, "I can hear you, can you hear me? I can see you, can you see me?"
I do, and I do, and I hold my breath till The Tempest is over and I can safely share the news,
"Caliban has left the building."

The Hanging Man muddles his way through the crowds near the exit, and with his one good foot waving in the air, squarks, "When shall we three meet again?"

"When sugar-Babiš melts in the warm, 'with it' Spring rain."

And how is it the message was not sent?
And how is it we say the same things?
And how is it we still believe there is a message to be sent, when we say the same things?

"Daddy, no! It's sunning too hard. I don't want to go out today. I am happy where I am. Besides we are all doing the same things. What is there to meet out there? What is there left to learn? It is sunning too hard and we are one."

Ken's shorts pumping like welcome blood-rushes through a haemophiliac's watery imagination. Claiming in all sincere surreality,

"Not the same! Not the same! No! Not the same!"

Bob holding my hand in the midst of this confusion; vulnerable and lending.
"David Černý will join our Isolation Collection, with his tanks and his bombs and his guns and his bombs."
Good for the left of things thingly.
But indifferent.
A roaring child in the street burning along with the fantasy cars ablaze; big smoke shadows in the Trója garden maze.

Do not fantasise too loudly.

And with the strength bestowed upon me by Gillian, Jo, David, Louis, Chantelle, Jessica, Hagai and Robert, I trust myself just enough to ferry across these troubled waters, bisweptually.
Colourful.
Pink mainly.
Loping, badbacked to the Legendary bard Lumír and the unsung Píseň.
The Dvůr Králové Manuscript prattles,
"Lumír refused to sing a hymn for the winners of The Maidens' War and sings instead his last song to Vyšehrad,"
then he is said to have Townshended his instrument in a furore of national contrivance.

I know someone who knows, so I know.

And the devil's stone broken in three.
I wait for you to message me.
No!
Not the same.
I will not have the same message.
I have no message.
I have hands you can hold. I have ears you can bend. I have masking tape, plus the really strong black gaffa stuff for important things.
Tape that could fix that devil stone.

Was a rotten trick anyway. The gambit was unwinnable.

Devil was duped,
which defeats the object.

There are good messages and bad messages
and neutral messages.
Three types.

And a coffin goes in this door and a married couple comes out this,
and indoors...indoors the neutral remain.
Cosplaying 'meaning'. Colourful. Black predominantly. But uncool black.

And all the single ladies on benches in the park are doing interviews on their phones. The morning, afternoon, evening benches waiting for their meal of first-loves and brass in-memoriams to give those 'loves' direction.

Probably no more than two 'important' things.
Maybe three.
The third thing probably neutral.
Probably.
And as for the millinillions of 'important' things our fellow earthlings worship in fitful panic and giddy awe, they would be better off flinging them into Krištof Kintera's studio and letting him preserve them in pots of paint for shits and giggles.

Circuit board municipalities and bouncy balls and marching twigs and photographs of the artist's very own floorplans to Atlantis.
An 'important' piece the critics will call it,
as the critic in turn is preserved in plastic.

'Important' artists bottled and tamed. 'Important' writers drunk and shamed. Impotent directors tucked away. The fruitful vying to be the fruit.
A.I. waiting in the wings for perpetuities' singular reboot.

A fresh walk to a cenotaph.
Broken pigeons in a turtle dove's bath.

Garbled questions from a toddler unlearned.
No answers for the toddler.
No. Not the same.
It's important that they ask. It's important you don't answer.

Crushing it with five hours to spare. The magic time.
All the time in the world.
Still not going to come up with the thing. The thing in itself.
The thing within.
Why do we think time can do it? It will be the same time four hours from now.

I lean forward, elbows on knees and stare at the floor, and think, 'A good time to let my thoughts just be.'
Let go.
The thoughts will out!
I don't let go.

"Scrunch your toes up in the carpet. It will relax you,"
the man sitting next to John MacLaine says in Die Hard.
The first one.
And he does. In the hotel. And it works.

It's not working. Never does. I do it again. My stomach is the voices. The streetlight comes on at eight pm.
Policed.
It is five pm. The lamp does not wait.
I'm in the dark. In the glass. In the blue.
Nothing 'out of the blue'.

The Czech Cabernet Sauvignon like comfort sex with a toothless paracetamolian.

TWENTY-FOUR

Namely names.

You, are an encyclopaedia, and the dogs of memory you walk eat from the palm of your pen. They turn on me.
Bite me. A child being bitten.
I am an adult afraid of being a child being bitten.

Confident twelve-year-olds make me nervous.
And bitey dogs.
The ghosts don't follow.
I have the memory of Disney Dory and diaries would confuse Fu Xi.

And gradually, as it became unimportant…it became important.

Rob Menefee apogee effigy sitting in my seat and exuding the 'good' I feel when I am in motion.
Twisted Spoons pressed in the mouths of the literature babes speaking a different Yazzyk.
They's all busy playing in the busy Trafika. Dave and I preoccupied with Ben's spicy vegetarian Chilli prelude to any sex encounter's rarefied rump.

"I'm leaving tomorrow. I wish I could meet you again when you've turned thirty."
A naked wink by way of a brazen, outback, backhanded compliment.

Christopher Morris, apogee pedigree, in the hot seat translating the forerunners of this revolution back into Czech before any of us are able to get ahead of ourselves. Four-eyed

pocket buttons in a beret keeps our hallucinating heads for us.
Clean cut literati with the cheeky predatory panache of a
pickled Hermelín.
The older little brother who came along to play, to see what all
the fuss was about and write about some day.

Baby-faced Andy Capp, Jeffrey Young and Ra Bob; Irish Noel,
Glen Melia;
Dennis the Menace prototypes hotWired into the main frame
of our hallucinogenic history,
huddled in all nine quarters of our library headings.

Míša Raven Raven, Cool Max, Uncool Max, Gwendolyn Albert,
Tim Otis, Lawrence, and Margot from 'Superman the Movie'
and 'Sisters' and Beck's musician friend, and the kid working
with Terry Gilliam got his signed tin of spam stolen from his
locker.

All we ever wanted was for something to happen,
and when it finally does,
you find out that your Dog Day Afternoon is nothing but a
missed curly-photo-opportunity-memory,
and you feel deep, weird and improvised and don't you know;
that's how you become famous in the first place?

A humourist cursed with a melancholy spirit
in the galley of the ship of fools 'playing' for a living.
Our futures sacrificed in order to be having a good time
and to be making stuff up
Colouring in,
rhyming things with other things. Laughing and joking and
making people cry for the sake of a moment's respite from all
this unwarranted guff.
And the sacrifice feels good. The fact of sacrificing affording
new joyous, Tolstoian sensations.

"And what of the political angles?"

While politics is avoiding the political, art is the only politics on
which we can rely.

Living through a moment in history. Envious of artists who
went to war.
So we battle our invisible enemies by doing what artists do best;
we sit alone, in a room, reading, crying
and inventing stories.

"What lies ahead of us is either greatness or total oblivion."
Dave also told me that he would like to die in the most
uncompromisingly embarrassing situation imaginable.

Bless.

No Jackanories bez Dave.
No this.

TWENTY-FIVE

"Louder! We can't hear a word!"

"*It is now more than ever (as always) every mother and father's sacred duty to alert their children to the ever-present danger, and to the friendly guise it is likely to assume. A little candy, a toy or an apple can suffice to lure an artist to their doom.*"

The diamond-shaped and swelling sweeps, clearly seen in the word 'swoon' reveal all.
"Your whole life has been a gap year."

Picking at the bones of future Mike's rotten corpse,
feeling confident that smashing in the teraformatted skull
of terra-informed earth's
cravated murderers of hope (myself included, and the Buddha, and Bugs Bunny) is a mission well worth

$1.70 cents; the estimated price of a two-minute Skype call to one's daughter, on earth, from a spaceship on some Kubrickian Odyssey.

Not one of us good enough to speak in terms everyone might comprehend without need of sedatives,
advertisement breaks
or that bit where a bunch of sexy strangers dance to music that would fail to make a rabbit twitch.

And you ask about politics.
I see your politics and raise you an anarchism sandwich
and a 550ml can of Kozel,
with 10% extra free.
Another consciousness-shifting monolith, but fizzy.

And the day it all changed was every day you ever thought to yourself, 'This is the day when things will surely change'.

Suits 'n' Shorts.
Champagne in Toby Jugs.
Cheap graffitied Limos.
An orchid for the homeless.
Life jackets for the starving.

Don't be a bore, give me a smile.
I'll see your sandwich and raise you fifty at the end of another wasted month.
You watch a lot of TV and movies and the close-up's always on you.
You read more than you watch TV or movies and the camera isn't a camera now, it's a house cat and it wanders for miles, among others of its kind, before it returns for its own furry close up.

And if you don't read, and you don't watch TV, you are a shiny, golden pony boy.
You are shiny golden, you.

1994 and 2023, years as lairy as Timothy Carey.

And if time is not made up of static moments but flows, then your photographs are infinitesimally small movies in our cluster,
which is cool.
And if time is not made up of static moments but flows, then your books don't make any sense and you've got blue eyes, you've got green eyes, you've got blue eyes, you've got brown eyes
and no, I'm just kidding, your eyes hover between blue and green,

which is nice.

"Okay?"
"Okay."

So the time tunnel yawns open and David Barnes builds a bridge between Paris and Prague.
Alex is here and Anastasia is here, and Marko and Jaromír and Tyko and Robert's with us too.
Robert's idea.
And Jo's here. And as the lights go off we are falling some of the time too.
And we drink.
And we cry.
And we fall and we fall.
Because we all need to know we are still so very alone.

Echoes at Obejvák from the rare pew.
A professionally speakeasy where we convivialed the evenings.
Grooming the baked spectatoes in Beseda Kolčavka.
Sleazy listening cocktail jazz to dilute the Mediterranean.

In the reading glasses of candlelight we flicker in front of each other.
Able-mouthed preach-things.
Expository Blush-Whackers.
Balabenka Badingadongs.
Elemental Watsons.

The takeaway, a screenshot of how to make a speaker.
Act when acting's called for and sit when feeling weaker.
When mood purports to pale you and your comrades wield their wicks
And your truths are not forthcoming in the throes of Braxton Hicks.

Sleeping melanchoholiac in the stood-up war room dead bed.
A Mother's Day gift unwrapped.
Poets smoked up gone home.
Just the ION-speaker-Road-Rocker, gas-station-wine, project space keys, conscionably loud music, dusty dust and me.

We dream of dark horses, black sheep and Danielle.
The white witch whispering her wells.
A wish-bat tossed into her life-giving springs of mischievous

glitter
And infernal promises smiling full canto.
We wake crying but cradled and missing the night.

TWENTY-SIX

Ready to build towards the reward.
You can too.

The reward that looks like a pulled pork sandwich wrestled
from the table of a crying Trump avatar secretly imbued with
everlasting sunshine and a heart the size of the tin man's leg
warmers;
and my teeth strong;
strong like chewing-a-small-private-plane strong.
I am in a turquoise, cricket-bat shaped flying saucer christened
by your gentle tread and starlight sensitivity.

All time in a bushel and a peck and the emotional well-being of
a moment's notice before we say anything which might come off
too clingy but is in fact adorable.

There's a shrinking Capulet made prominent misread wrist
porn.
There's a raining Late Show we haven't yet seen yet.
There's a thousand musicals I am resolved to write with the
help of your honeyed, songbird beauty and crisp, lioness high
notes.
I am all the ten story love songs for you.

"Ya Mek me want ta be a bitter moon.
Don't get me wrong. I fucking love moons."

Discovering Jo's work like a tipsaholic carousing for a handhold.
And one two three, she focalised me,
and three four five, slapped me sold, saved, seen and alive.

"Maidin mhaith, (MA DJIN MWAH) beautiful! Let's team up

and see what damage we can do!"

Mid lockdown gallery visits rarified unt Faustian.
DSC with these mutant penises
and I can't talk to any of them.
And there's a carrot which is a penis, and there's a roll which is
a penis, and a submarine penis banging against our heads with
our masks as protection so we don't get pregnant whilst under
the influence of Černý's girlfriend in cool black lycra legs,
and there's this 2-metre squared replica of a 2-metre squared
vagina too,
plus the guilt of living away from my family all this time.
And the guilt of leaving my sister behind.
And all the sisters and brothers and friends left behind leave
a mark on the cold Czech ramparts and mad dogs' judgement
calls beside the mock seaside beside the mock sea.

And Chris said to me, "You're not a fucking teacher, man! You're
a writer! I'm going to take you under my wing!"
And I'm thrilled and I'm flattered
and Dad said,
"If I had the chance to do it all over again, I wouldn't have kids,
no. No, sir. No kids."

Belly voice preach-preach.
"Don't do it, kiddo! Finish what you began."

Two pages a day for a hundred days and a penny for your
thoughts as you run out of space and delete unnecessary apps
till the messages come flooding in,

"Where exactly did you 'begin' anyways?"

We is down to the residuals, but better late than never,
and better worse than dead,
and better same than better?

"Why you got to make lists all the time? What you Gotta make
all these comparisons for? S'wrong with you?!"

I want to write down all the sounds we make that are universally understood,
but it's impossible.
There is no word for ————.

I will film the sounds and post them as posterity videos.
Watch this spaceman.
The Great Unreadable Novel for Universal Ocular Consumptives.
And a book where every word is in quote marks.

The Roadster quiet. Dust settled.
An early head full of swine.
Lihovarská 12.
Kids and their parents shuffling to the kindergarten past the frosted glass windows of this old car repair shop.
Kladno 20 D,
the blue, iron pillars protecting me from imminent collapse and an Obejvákian propulsion to bigger and greater things.
Paleontologging in and out of a fitful sleep.
Paying money in dreams to have bolder ideas. Visualising the work of an obscurer other.
'I could pretend that work is mine,'
and it makes me sick. And I make a universal sound.

Strength in numbers.

"It will be a bridge from this building across to the apartments, but the bridge will look like a train crashing into the side of the building."
I know.
"David will make it."
I know. I've seen his penises.
"Your time here is limited."

Gathering the wine corks to hurl at the nosey children poking their heads through the studio door for a looksee at Andrew Goodall's garden spades with which to bury the Blossoms' delightful cover of The Beatles' Paperback Writer and his long-walk-clouds mathematical, and his rustless concepts, and his chosen words, and his hangman rope, and his photography gangs' warm alphabet soup.

The Last Picture Show. A quiet unlikely crew, isodrifting in and out of view, bubbling gently as conversation comes to after a smack on the head, and all of your friends and your family finally understand you.

"Can I please park here until the apocalypse is over?"

Muzak throttling the life out of the salads; dire soft rock become wafer thin ballads. Universal groan as a bontemps organ-blinder fists 'Come Together' into a weeping shadow of its former self.

TWENTY-SEVEN

Fully charged and sundry flirting.
Bipartisan semi drunks;
Dave skates-to-live.

Pivnice U Kata for want of a won't. We are post-rub-structures
and mouldy, loaded Akela's from a Skautský institutionalised
Kafka-trauma,
one too many Jamesons and a forgotten Tarot spread.

Managing drinking tours in my head, where we retread the
haunts we haunt.
Where everybody knew our names long before a gaggle of
drunks was obliged to label itself a creative collaborative.

The Derby a breeding ground for bodhisattvas and jelly-mould
breakdowns.
All blooms.
All that were buried in that dead land
destined to sprout mainly years afterblogs,
and gonorrhoea renaissanced.

We who remain, 'The Walking Said',
milking the situations where we're better off than dead.
We who cluster in retrospect-idyllic of the concrete potential
reinforced by our enviable absence of cause.

"Remember how those we aspire to be, recorded for posterity
their times?"

Let's copy and paste, and change the names, then back to our
fun and games.
Why go to all the trouble of reinventing the literary batons

which have failed to capture the minds of the mulberry goons,
make us spit and stab in badly lit, badly ventilated, badly
peopled skive dives?

Sailor's piss streams dribbling through the alley-air shaft
connects She-I's pulling some lazy perpetrator's cock.
Sullied gifthorse in the basement of U Krále Jiřího.
Hair-a-mess. Ego ruffled.
Hairy legged romance on a rented pedalo.
Mating to a rainy joystick party of two tempesting yoopsters.
Wheeling around the beauty with a tacky dash of nature
unbecoming a candied cad,
delusional frustrator, whimpering post-coitally.

"Don't even bash or baste 'em, just peel, chop and put them in
a hot oven like that. They go crispy. And fluffy inside. I swear to
God!"

"Take it. Take his card, you fool!
Who's Robert? Robert's a famous photographer!"

And there are benefits to not speaking the language.
Benefits that befit a battered bard.
One dream-hears the null honorifics of blasé tram beings,
post office neo clerks, supermarket blabber grannies
and propels them to adequate discussion jockeys mainlining
the collective ego structure.
Nothing overstated,
nothing undersaid,
nothing hurtful to the senses, but elementary notion lotions to
a bus-riding cynic-jerk.
Self-proclaimed jerk jerks.

They all blossomed, shall we say, for the sake of Prargument;
each and every dunkin' slab of them.
All the Dodgers, all the second strikers, knuckle-shamers.
Muscle-tongued, level two Paladins, and they lean soft on the
gender bias of a lemon-flavoured debate team.

The reflection-stomach of my Cartman-raped android

rationalises the embarrassment of three tea-leaf likes and a solitary heart for all that hard work.
True karate is never in your tummy.
You will find true karate undressing in the dojo of your third eye. Now let's get to know him,
plug him,
sell him
and give that man a hand-job.

And while he was waiting and while they were waiting and while she was waiting, the rainfall bristled as she watched him from a safe distance penning their ode to French cheeses.

We had no phones, no internet and no cheddar to call our own. But we could quote the path of the riotous man whilst being beset on all sides by the inequities of the selfish and the tyranny of high school bullies.

"Daddy, Daddy, Daddy, why didn't you teach me to punch?
Daddy, Daddy, Daddy, why didn't you teach me how to take a punch?
Mum......Mum......Mum............Mum..................................
Mum......"

TWENTY-EIGHT

All hail the Balabenka Badingadong!
The pustules for free.
The galloping gourmet got Tetris.

"We will fix it. We will mend it. We will fix it. We will mend it."
"I mean who knows what language he speaks?"
"We are living the wrong way."
"Dying for a retirement."

Chantelle Goldthwaite and Jessica Serran
(names saved to change the innocent)
gather me together in their arms and put me back together
again.
Right ways.
The Canadian ambassador tying my fate to a side of me I
thought buried beyond watering.
Artists birthing.
Mothers,
and single ladies
and just ladies
warming themselves at the doorstep of perspective, at the feet
of the sun, at the helm of all phases of the moon
and Vltava boat races.

Hold...19...hold...29...hold...39...hold...
ENOUGH! Now show your work!

Boycotting Nod gallery forever and no day-jobs this lifetime.
The high bar of hope they beat us with
after pinky promises made.
But libel-licentiously the Canuck begat us
and we begat 'Identity' (the theme of our strap-on)

and our identities begat begetting and a serious amount of first-bloodletting.

Ex-Post adding hocs to a DudeBabe for life in the shape of a Goldthwaite-barmy come comrade come softly come toast queen.
Bug raising storm annihilator,
chartreuse dope empress.
Leggy Mountbatten of the Alt-Art Societal fortress constructed with googly eyes and formal pyjama bottoms.
Cutting the head off all curatorial Samurai with the swish of her sharpie tagged skateboard,
juggling them into a multilingual drum,
pounding the shit out of all that has been and ritualising every approach of all that is to come.
So much to be done, so little crime.
As the fires blaze around her California home she Skypes 'NOW!' in the face of the manifestos we trace, and we feel sorry for the ones who come last in any race.

Competition is for
...the unsure.

The Alt-Art Society all inclusive.
We will not judge.
We will not hide.
We will not won't.
The Threshold defence – We promise to protect this Threshold with all of our condiments.

Good day ladies. Good day, sweet ladies. I doff my black spray-painted, Marks and Sparks cap to you with all the fabric woven in England by the light of our five petalled moon.

And the blonde jogger-in-a-bag making her third round of my Vyšehrad fort walls sense-recalls the effort it takes to keep a partner interested.
All heil the Balabenka Badingadong! Bob bless you ladies, I cuddle have done it without you. Woken. Relevanted. In your debt.

Yes. Yes. I promise to stay fit.
My cholesterol only went up by a tiny bit.

We walk and we talk and me cardio is Delbossed by your encouraging battles.

1420 medieval cloister a-la Pendragon.cz.
Doorstep re-enactments of bygone stage re-enactments.

I've got thirty crowns. Enough for an ice cream.
Not enough for a sausage.

I wonder if chamber music really sounded like that.
Reading Philip O'Neil's Mental Shrapnel I fact check myself.
Did even I sound like that back then, when I was medieval and you could buy wooden toys and rustic buns and a Langoš cost less than a whizz in the park.

I'll google Šárka when I get home and see what she did to these guys; twenty foot tall and bladder-free.
Jo mentioned something about Šárka's actions being a tad excessive and this IS exactly what gods would have looked like, neo-demo(N)cratically.
Ugly words.
Bad words!

I-Statue and a mock fight begins.
I-Statue and am weary of competition.
How to win the maiden's hand without becoming the fame of the land?
Sensitivity and fairness will only get you so far, with a maiden who judges a man by his car.

A saddled horse, a blind-folded eagle, a fire-red Ferrari and a hunting beagle.

The players take their places. Willie Watson makes funny faces.
I'm down on fights and races.
I discovered a better way to tie shoelaces.

Organise your day, the Lockdown 'experts' say.
Prepare for your middle-ages.
Programme on a blackboard if you have one.
Dress for your role, exercise, be fair, stay positive,
Skype, Zoom, rearrange your room into something resembling a local pub.
Play hospoda sounds and put sport on the box.
Plan your next exhibition for NTK, NG or DOX.
Think big in your limited space.
Finally we are all running
at exactly
the same
pace.

Šárka had her reasons. She needed to be in the town where they knew what she was like and didn't mind.
Ctirad's sacrifice slid upright and copacetic and not a cobra's bite away from a Jaws movie t-shirt on a seven-year-old male chauvinist prig.

Suck my dame college funds away from us before we gets 'head 'f ourselves.
Death at the bottom of a bottle and a recyclable revenge as ghost porn exes draw you to the cliffs and mark their territory with a tourists' bear trap.

I understand why infants and toddlers scream so much.
It's not for no reason, but for the praise of sound and the engulfing hug we are shy to take advantage of.
Paperback writers know its benefits.
I write what my father cannot help but say by the second, daily.

If you listen real close to the page, you will hear
one,
long,
drawn out scream.

And yes, even though you are beautiful and yes, even though I will spend the rest of my laughter and heavy sighs on you, I

reserve the right to burst.
In front of you.
In public. Just like you.
I will die for you.
There is nobody like you.
I know when I am low. And if I have to raise my hands high above my head to keep you from the quicksand I will.
Won't rest till Gandalf, Deus ex Machina, strides by with his knotty staff and pulls you from the muck of your outside influences and borderline questions.

I glisten when you drink. I shine when we drink together.
I would that we could fall into each other's armies right now and drink a truce to all our minds' giddy soldiers.
I am incinerated. I am incarcerated.
I was sad. You rescued me.
Blood brother/sister lighting the way through an unwelcoming tunnel of trouble.
I will not let you do this alone.
I will never stop typing ... ...

Mr Bin knows.
All here in black and white and the blur between the thresholds and 'this' is imperceptible how we know there ain't no left and right
or up and down.

And now!
And now?

And now?

TWENTY-NINE

There's scooters and umbrellas and grass
and I am wearing a light grey cap
and a baseball shirt.
I touch the table and look at my fingers but forget to feel the table.
My playlist is beginning to irritate me.

Instant Karma is fucked up, even when it's beautiful.

Logan's Lovecraftian musical pre-sent in youse blues.
Samira, Samantha and Mar Von Zellen;
inspiration for indescribably squamous bouts of spooky
eldritch and diabolical, timely self-reflection aimed at a
lyricless victim of nauseating rebukes.
I cut my losses and run for the wings.

"Eventually you won't need the Tarot cards. The cards are training wheels. You will soon see them all around you."

Patience, diligence and perseverance.
Silent traces of balance discouraged by influences we make
pinhole cameras from and bow and curtsy and continue.
We didn't freeze when you hosed us off,
we picked up our packs like good soldiers and held on.
Ants first.

Each one of us dealing with outbreaks of confidence differently.
Brain damaged kings
and outspoken obscurants planting burnt out afternoons in the good place.
Brilliance in big night Bolt shouting 'Reverse! Reverse!"
like Kora in purgatory

and a husband in an ice-box who could never speak his mind.

A poets' fracas in a conceptualist's flat.
In the red corner, Prague's unwreathed laureate,
and in the blue,
a complete and utter twat.
All knives out.
All colours bled.
All worlds' words recycled and dreamed in black and white and quiet eggs.
Buddhas mistreated by bikini-clad editors.
The publishing house goes bye-bye after one garbled invite
from real life aliens.

In cuneiform Enheduanna clarifies the Malkmus.

The preliminary scarlet letters under reception-muffled voice.
No microphone necessary
but undivided attention, and no, no more than ten people
standing at this mass protest.
If the government chooses to close the borders this Monday, I
don't know how I will survive without you.
Our own attentions divided in these sunning Autumns which
we will not share if the economy don't bolster and the polar
regions melt and the heart of this age scrolls down too fast to
see that there is plenty still on Netflix which we haven't yet seen,
and Planeta Česko is a Moneyball Bullitt in a Duney Incal.

Now crush that ice, guess my weight, tune that guitar and kill all
Republicans, advertisers, horse flies and gospels.
There is no poetry in a Hijab.

"Woman, life, freedom

and death to ALL dictators!"

THIRTY

Batter up, Dave.
First over the top of the wage-clad-dads.
Needling dishes and waiting on
in vinegary aspect.
Fakhreldin! Pride of the Religion run out by the monetaries.
"Ya can stick yer lousy job!"
Chased by a knife wielding cantaloupe guesses customers'
dietary needs,
"Horny? Hummus!
Sleepy? Spinach!
Shy? Shish Kebab!
like a fairground barker guessing the weight of spouses.
Never an ounce over Babylon
and good luck with that.

Milking the whispered orange night into our expansive
heartburns
and fiddling the shops for beans.
We balustraded our happenstance and fortified with fats.
Discussed bringing suits back into fashion
and filling Rohlík's with Sunday roasts. 'Dave and Mike's
Sensible Foods', soon him big cheffed in Cornucopia.
Sleeping on shelves post dawn clap trappery.
Elementing Lady Diana's demise with a Tomato Soup surprise.
Jungmannova gurgling yanks' ethical barometers in sardonic,
white, permanent obscurities.

Collaborated with the homeless, the gormless,
the feckless social gizzards;
and, at a dollar a pop, tripped for weeks in sweating bunkers.
Gargled anti-sceptics and spat 'em in the river.
Played hopscotchwhisky on burning decks

and pranced with all the flamers firing.
Gurgitating LSD memes prior to the 11:11am Saturday 26th of September rain.

My hands are shaking and I can't feel my feelings.
This godless twerp is in for it now.
The keystone.
The pulchritudinous pivot.
The choicesyoumake.
Andthereyouare.
And there you are again, at square one one one one.
Capsules out of the atmosphere.
Door hinges loose.
Black matter lives.

See you under the powder Tower.
Hand-standing showboats grounded.
Landlocked mermaids and mermen gobbing on each other against all regulations in an attempt to wake this third mentality.
Blunt knives out.
We butter each other up and madly stab at corona bellies till apotheosis.
All we ever really wanted.
And Love Before Breakfast.

No Sen Qua Nunnery for you, my dear.
I handle the seven embers so you don't have to.
But do have to ask your permission before I paint you black with the charcoal remnants of a Smíchov fire that burned so brightly.
Make you infinitesimally small. Fit you in my capsule.
Unseen, but still so verythere.
Sensitive, unprovable.
Moved,
and unmoveable.

The patriarchy climaxes a hypothetical distraction modus operandi – Down with Effigies.
No escapism once you've escaped.

Microscopes for contact lenses and rom-coms duly fact-checked.
No love light for Plutonic migrations cum fly-by reprimands for forgetting to dot.com the I.
Or not, I can't remember.

The principle product of Myopia – the laughter of a village idiot.

Your furrowed brows will meet across a crowded room and you will labour till Jupiter's moons have their seventy-nine multilingual partners.
Coulda bin a bird of prey.
Coulda bin a rock star.
Coulda bin a loner.
Andthenshesmiled.
Nanny Sleep and her quagmire of chrome domes leaped trabant to trabant to 'The Shining' soundtrack,
and belched out the devil's alphabet to a hungry class of dyslexic non-believers.

"What you gonna call it if it ain't love?"
"A ghost story."

So who did you think you knew you knew?
Your god is not my god.
How did you die? I know you told me. I had been drinking. Tell me again.
How did you die? You didn't die?! I'm sorry, I completely misunderstood.
I thought you had died. Crazy!
So you didn't. Okay.
So...where were we?

Do you go to church?
I act.
Do you have a belief?
I act.
Do the dead bother you? When you thought I was dead you seemed perturbed. Did it make you want to believe?

No. I got a big bookshelf, and I know better than to get rattled by doubt.
You act?
I do.
Do you act good?

Book shore. Sea deep. Bloke-bred, spoon fed, scared of nothing but nothing.
Got superhero legs and a smokin' hot bod',
and the kill-skills of a neighbourly cop.
Please don't forsake me. I need more and that's all our fault.

Let me take you on a trip.
A big diamond.
Just give in.
Card sixteen isn't such a leap.
Now, get off my base.
Time to run.

We are Charlie.
We have Charlie.
We are all writing the same book.
The book that will lead to the end of religion as we know it.
Not nosebleed fast but I'm laughing with a gun
and I think I am the one
and I need to be stopped with the smallest words because
believers don't read right and have been lied to
and look like you but shine within the colourless hope of a
Czech politician's wet dream.

Zeus is well dead.

But your teachers stabbed me
and burnt me
and hung me
and tortured me.
Your teachers whose quotes you jot down in holy cowed leather notebooks and memorise in order to sound wholly holy.
They is gods?
I'll pull your teeth out.

They is gods?
I'll flay your skin from your body.
Your teachers rape.
Your teachers murder in the name of salvation.
Your teachers' teachers are demons.

We are writing the same book in your words.
Making the same art on the same radio waves.
First wave slaked.

There's been a giant bug on my window for three days straight.
National gallerists come for Tarot readings in the rain
and Peter Parker's impatient to just be a normal kid again.
Jessica and Branislava and Chantelle curious and singular in
their goals and remixes. Listen carefully and you can hear them
today...live feeds.
Marvellously ladies in embryonic purpose positive.

Pay the money
and hold them close. You won't regret it.
No shame in asking for help when you ain't seen a collector in a
month of Spotified Sundays.
Keep your sass in the studio, nobody likes a whiner.
Things aren't going the way you planned?
Cop on, strap on, wash yourself and rubber up.
That bug didn't write itself.

We've been dying for their stone-faced lies,
so open up,
grow up
and SHOW UP!
These women shit you not,

I shit you not.

THIRTY-ONE

So Jessica is all moderation with a bag full of weapons of Miss destruction
and ammunition enough for three more world wars.
She's a brass neck and leads us into battledress,
embracing fear like a thirteen-year-old teenage boy embraces
the receipt for the sex worker birthday present from his fucked up cowboy Dad.

"Boy, you is a man now!"
"Dad, you is a fool!"

Do not be afraid to wear whatever makes you shine.
If we moved out of the city we would miss out on all this inspirational dirt-dirt.
I am not going anywhere without my yellow Wellington boots,
red/white striped bloomers,
bin bag tee and Moroccan tablecloth stroke pirate hat.

You drop your attitude as soon as you enter that skirmish, seeeeee,
and you pull down your ego and drop it in the mud, seeeee
and wibble your way forward like a newborn giraffe for a kilometre or two
and there's Branislava to pick you up and stabilise you
and give you a few nibbles
and a tell you a story to warm your cockles
and you buck up and thank god you're alive
and she spins you round till your nibbles reanimate and she points you in no particular direction but covers the tram fare.
Let's the chaps down the line know you are going to be there eventually.
"Take your time. Don't be stingy. You got an idea? Do it. Have

the courage to change, and the difference to know the matter.

Don't
be
stingy."

Stomping through all the other felchers' egos sloppy and
melting into the fields you perambulate screaming for your
Mother.
And that's fine, that's fine, you's a soldier now, kiddo.
And in that field there's some grass,
and in that grass there grows a tree,
and in the tree there's a nest,
and in that nest there's an egg,
and in that egg in the nest in the tree in the grass in the field of
egos is a note.

"Dear Sicko, love it. Perfect. Please send me the whole file. I will
send you some more pictures to inspire you. DudeBabe."
I cop on
Strap on
Wash
Rubber up
Grow up
and
SHOW UP!

And I look like a tempestuous, flamboyant Rambo playing
Public Enemy too loud in my leopard skin, Princess Leia
headphones
the size of the ulcers Jessica cut right out of my stomach.
And Jo's all pan-fried, with soy sauce, mustard, honey, lemon
and Nando's hot'n'sweet sauce.

There's still time for Coca Cola to buy into the weed generation
and Goldthwaite.
But don't advertise it.
I kill all you motherfuckers.
Pull the children's teeth straight out of the poplars and load up
my toothpaste gun; spray that shit at everyone.

It's like this y'all
Like this y'all
And you don't stop.

Scratch to fade out, and a light snowfall.
We see from the attic windows the savage cultures clashing in
an attempt to get back into their universal onesie and finally
binge The Wire and Bohm's Theory of Wholeness.

We are Everyman
at the Souterrain tables.
Dry year copulating fingerbanging hand twins.
Samira in good voice as I pick myself up from the curb they
last saw me, and empty into her ears my magazine of the finer
points of Iranian calligraphy.

Disconnect.
Bad timing.

And at eight,
another evening of the finest expo of private cabin moment
expositions of histories that rhyme, some of the time.
Performing colourants approved by the W.H.O. shared in
shy equanimities at close proximities and you can still smoke
here after ten because of some forgotten/remembered Terry
Cashman loopsong.
Aliens cluster like Mick Jagger gangster hot rods twisted by
their own press and vices and friendly Souterrain prices.

Aureliuses illustrated by a hungry, mad yank apologising for
being from hungry, mad America,
then holding out his hand for some change with which to
change.
A cold beer and a warm Yelp.
Being underground these days is meeting by accident and
sticking around for the nuptials.
Consummation of the gathering forty days and a Naked Snack;
you pick the nits from my hair

and I'll store all your Wintery tyres.

Carnalising retweets.
Caramelising ants.
There's more than twenty ways to name a cat.

Snap, Crackle and Pop turn ShitKid up, and on, and grin at the eggy faced Monkees surrounding the scene.
Ping – Surrogate!
"ShitKid 'liked' my post! ShitKid liked MY post!"

This dance will last forever.

THIRTY-TWO

So Thor's banging on about the 'peripherals' we are damaging
and Sebastian is holding his own up on the stage,
Wolfe-trod by graphomaniacs in their primest Chianti ego
balaclavas.
Cheap Shots and Wilde claims to be uploaded and pod cast
into the space we would be jealous of if we didn't hold such a
grudge against it.
No snap on these now book shores but fame,
alone and thinking,
'Wouldn't it be nice. Wouldn't it be lovely; summer only you
and I, and to hell with all these defensive quotations.'

Only three little words really count.
Partners in Crime.

Vít collecting,
Vít collective
and word-rashed languishes within avant-garde techno trances
formulated into district poesy columns make the whole aspect
fancier.
He calms the quoth and Blakes the backdrops,
handshooks like a humane, and humanes like a Taroted lion
queen.
Relinquishing dictation models to the all-forgiving magnet
in which we all joined
unapplied, which he gets,
like a maserati 'gets' a racecourse, or a chip gets a butty, or a
cloudy body of water hinting at its own imperceptible weight by
showering its love on bodies born to wink gets a wink.

How to make the devices we devise work in all our favour.
Standing on one webbed foot with three socks on,

this Maverick spills lighter fluid all over his write hand and
whoosh! Lordy! Leaps out of those sockses and buys up all the
rivers of slivovice Pryor to the flood.
They'd call it a reboot if it didn't sound so similar.
They'd call it familiar if it didn't sound so suše.

Soused on the Pivní Domeček roof roof.
Becoming Artist alternates,
birthing protoactive firsthand Karlovo Náměstís.
Opening with Big Bang pockets o'cans slipped in the gallery
kitchen.
Cocktail progenitor grimace.
Grimace pins us down
like drinky-dead butterflies with a lengthy tale of the three
blind liqueurs.
The beer goggles split between us. One googly eye each,
bringing out the bubbles hiding inside all melancholy
DudeBabes.

WYWH, making the rounds.
We lead these streets profounder.
Oh, teach me how to smoke those doobies you do.
Piss everyone right off with one of our big bong IN jokes.
Tag every flyer with an 'ALT-' and walk coolly away
like sexy action heroes from a very expensive Hollywood gas
station explosion.

And if the whisky he poured was an ocean
and we were turtle doves,
the plough men who rhapsodise over their plump young wives'
lamb tea
would captain us to the depths
and tie yellow ribbons round our happy corpses.

'Saved myself for you'.

The Strangeness of Her Beauty; beach-combing scavenger,
junk yard, second hand, antique wizard's lair, Egyptian tomb
raiding punker alchemist turns baubles of the quotidian into

enchanting visual mysteries only the viewer holds keys to.

'A man who believes in God can never find God.'

And Jessica turns to future Mike and asks,
"Is there a difference between what a piece of art means and what it does?"
Dox's Reduced Visibility of Ordinary Things.

Stanko-Sequens parallels
between the sculpted works of S&S
and Sadofsky-Trantina.
S&S, gorgeous, twisted Dr Seusses with O.C.D. I.M.O.
S&T, randy, cocky, fucked up Brothers Grimmmmmm,
bollocksing their way across the senate floor,
bending the truth uglypretty
like tabloidian newpaperists.
The critic in me winced at not having the courage to be quiet.
'Believing' all I say.
Wanting to believe the things I say.
Sharing my boobs in church.
And S&S are T&T and S&T are P&D and as much a plague of enlightenment as they are a spoken word instrumental.

"Do you believe in God?" the interviewer asked Carl Jung.
"I don't believe," Carl replied. "I know."

To teach Helena the Tarot in Venice Beach
soon as the gestapo return her visa.
A silent sigh for Petr's chilli and his penchant for electric dogs.
The climbing frame of their imaginations punctuated with
bean bags filled with the dead foetuses of wannabe gladiators.
Dan spooling out smiles for some deepless airbags, kneehigh
to Pedja Djakovic tickling the ivories at Joe Strummer's shrine
built into the teeth of the Mount Rushmore hellboys.

The Ruttles, the inverse of folk art's Mad Power.
But the purpose.
Comedy, the volatile Molotov in the underrated hands of grinning idiots.

Propane originalities wriggling out from the limited chrysalis prints of a new Dada freak show.

"What do you paint?" Jessica asks.

Th In Gs Th At Li Ft Me.

THIRTY-THREE

Hagai begat Zvi begat begettings in commonly gots.
A surprise octogenarian, Nabdinian soulmate you just don't
return from a studio from.
Zvi and Eva Tolkovsky begat a Kat,
KNOW how to live and they know how to hug
and their Ron Weasley kitchen,
and their tables table-topped with 'This is what it's all about'
food, family and friends.
Zvi and Eva know.
They don't believe.
They know.
You just don't come back from a home like that.
Handsome daughter, rustic, farmstead garden kiln, ageless
charm, easeful manners, brass tacks, strong backs,
tinctured canine, collage lunches, welcoming depths,
calming presence, childlike curiosity, loving generosity.
Scrumpy with Rosie.
Some
Thing
To
Be.

Hagai set to evolve and or Möbius.
A Secret Santa in casual proofs predating the shoe shuffle of a
dancing worder.
A Good worder.
A Fine worder.

The isolation Collection hiatus-conducive
since we got no fucking choice
and this virus is as slippery as an unfinished simile.
Four four leaved clovers promise better times to come.

Although Jo tells me four leaved clovers don't mean shit.

I will alternate between the sun and Prague nine.

I dressed badly for the year.

Go ahead, confiscate me.
Put me to better use.
See into my head.
Clearly you're clear.
No conflicting information.

Re-record until the tape is garbled, chewed, weak;
no fear of specifics rearing their pustulated mugs in this
hovercraft full of eels.
But for Zvi.

All of history trembles on the surface of each newly ancient
canvas.
All of humanity clings desperately to every coltishly assembled
statue.
East and West collide in a seductive orgy of colour, lust
and hopeless hope.
Mutant Mickeys berate nazi zombies
whilst conjuring war scarred airships to escape the noose.
Disney porn relieves itself in mucky landscapes
of collateral damage.
Charred alchemists turn typewriters into architecture and
rewrite our psychic infrastructures.
Paddling through the bloody water tank of rescued objects,
the heart is visited by a familiar phantom.
We recognise its features only after we have clawed at its
impossible visage
and agreed to lather on the UV protection
and bask in the nuclear sun of Tolkovskian dystopian
paradises.

Mushroom clouds hover, promising brief acid rain repose.
A 5D cinema complete with electric chairs.
Augmented surreality will coax the frightened adult back into

the courageous infant they once were.
A new old Jerusalem in the clogged arteries of Prague's labyrinthine underground.
A United States of umbilical fantasies.
A handspike hitch.
A figure of eight.
An overhand sheep shank and a concubine's grey chagrin.
Sandpaper scenes of unmuffled screaming.
Filthy leather gags of the tortured dipped in sailor's coffins filled with rum and cum and urine to paint an individual stinking flag for every child born.
His church is his act.
His message is his age.
His truth is his laugh.
His breath is his fear.
His strength is his hug.
His eyes are his hands.
His body is every body.
His life is his family.
His friends are his studio.
His studio is his student.
His student is his teacher.
His home is his breath.
His breath is your breath.

THIRTY-FOUR

And you can still smell Andre Breton's hair gel in the Mánes Exhibition Hall on Žofín island.
And the ink dripping from the Prague love letters of Eugène Émile Paul Grindel, aka Paul Éluard,
name changed to pave innocence.
Recited poetry in the City Gallery on benches on which whom
I room between Knihovna-kept copies
of Armand and Vichnar.
The post-curses to their weevil-twins a century unpacked.

And all welking in the foolscaps of Wilhelm Albert Włodzimierz Apolinary Kostrowicki, aka Guillaume Apollinaire,
name battered to pieces by a stray French Duke De What'sSoWrongWithBert?

There are places I remember and some are real.
The Royal Hospital Kilmainham in Dublin
and the Letohrádek Hvězda in Bílá Hora.
It was in the latter that I first met the Royal governor, Archduke Ferdinand on the very day of the Starry castle opening.

Obora, Obora,
Oh Hvězda, Hvězda
Obora,
Oh Hvězda
Oh Ferda,
Oh, Michael.

1558,
just past the yard arm,
time enough to grab a bubbly from beneath Fillipa's herbal

remedies
and transport myself into the future
where I might put the willies up André Breton in a 1935.
Habsversion of reincarnal 'Haven'twemetbefores?'

Yes.

June 1994.
The hottest summer in 'real' history.
My heterosexual life partner's Night of the Over-Ripe Bananas,
Purging Dadaism of all surreality,
and sending the 'Nine Forces' to Billa with a list of groceries
and condiments to pick up.
André asks for my autograph in blood
and I fob him off with something about an alcoholic's aversion
to parting with the rude Red stuff.
Jaroslav Seifert runs up in jodhpurs and asks us
"Where's the party at?"

"Go straight on to The Flying Octopus, take a right at The
Phantom Flan Flinger and keep going till you arrive at Issac
Bashevis Singer. Then drrrrrrrop!"

"Buzerante!" cries he back to us
as he hot tails it away along the invisible tracks of Magor's
Parallel Polis to his eighteen-hand high-horse
and,
after a fashion,
a call for the rebirth of the death of truth.

"We are the Second Culture," I assure André who is busy
picking Ferdinand up out of another burning bush screaming,
"There! There! I told you so, you heathens!"
We buy him a beer
and buchty s mákem
and take him back-back to the 15th century AIL
(after the invention of his lord).

And oh but back at the lodge the citizens' shenanigans would
have made the Devil-Man of Charlie's Bridge blush!

Here's Anna of Bohemia bedding Chaucer ad librium,
while in the fifth alcove of the six-pointed star
we spy Jan Hus mounting Wycliffe on poppers cultural!
And there's Shakespeare nostalging Bohemian Ginsburbia via
Arcimboldo's codpiece to Kafka,
to Klima(X)!

And Ferlinghetti dies this week 169169 days in the future to
googles of his best'uns come shared, liked, sad-face memorials.
We pull paper crowns from our Christmas crackers in the
summer palace,
and in honour of the City Lights proprietor and his drinky-
thinky poetry, we each wear our crowns unironically the whole
rest of the day.

In the entrance hall I see...is it Clark Kent? Is it Alan Levy?
stroking his collegiate.
Ego day-tripping Uber Humans spewing coin-bits into their
sweating paddocks
on the left bank of the nineties,
on a float, sailing me down the Vltava
of a street sword swallower's dreams.
Alan, the Jor-El lookalike of our new frontier.

"No, no, we are not just here for your super cheap beer. And it
hurts, I say it hurts when you mark us with this worn-out cliché,
and so, and so, and so Czechians beware!
Don't you know your words can wound a worder?"

"...somewhere within each of us here, we all know we are living
in a historic place at a historic time.
Future historians will chronicle our course – and I have reason
to believe that they're already here."

I throw up so I can have more of everything. Sic.

In search of the seventh point,
Bruce Sterling disagrees with this sentiment.

"...there is no André Breton here. People do sit and write – stop

by the Globe – scribbling busily in their notebooks. Many
American wannabe writers here – but there is no Prague
Literary Movement – No Prague literary-isms."

I think contrapuntal Cyberplink missed the punt!
Could not he see how gorgeous we all were?
Could not he see the magisterial timelines gathered in shiny
beer-cheeked orgy sat in the silent hum of this collusion-
solution
who are now accumulating our ploughed shares
and reaping the Krishnamurti of it.
Could not he?

And Rothko was fifty and Newman was fifty and De Kooning
was fifty before any of them had a one man show,
and in one month's time I will be fifty
with the skinny brained addle of a 0,5 l Alk 4,2% obd
warm tunnel vision.

A wrongfully arrested development,
tree-top contested
and sunburnt on only the right side of my prettyyy prettyyy
prettyyy face.
The literary-isms awoke now in a molasses profusion
of sympatico giddies and one or five seriosos,
two or four musikants
and seven or nine dilettantes.

So Mark Divo turns up with his sentient socks tucked into his
sandals-sense and fifth column Dadaist pyjamas.
Tote bags loaded but not drunk yet.
Andy knows of him.
Ferda asks Mark where the bar is.
Philippine fishes out her purse. Mark accepts the fishes.
Mark leads us by his blockchain to the living room we never
knew we had.
Prague is his living room, Invalidovna his Deacon Blue.
Building a ten-foot-long Kazoo, lit just so,
in the dark,
next to the W.C.

"Just pop a few crowns in the tumbler, I ain't counting, I trust you and you trust me because even though we just met, family is my policy."
"Who her?"
"She's a show girl."
"Who he?"
"That's a show man, man."

Every party is the last party and don't call it a party,
call it...unity.
Call it fucking Dignity.

THIRTY-FIVE

And round the corner prowls Jo (například),
Cleopatra calling!
One and two and three too beautiful saline, feline, divine,
capitulates to grand piano thong thongs
talking straight and getting it right so you don't have to.

Art procured from a history of her own making
and a party you want to be invited to.

And you never see the sausage being made. You should never
see the sausage being made. The sausage just appears like that,
one day, fully formed
and succulent
and exactly the way you imagined her;
that epiphanic when you stayed up all night in search of the
Yeti,
and you imagined your very own personal towering inferno
that would blast you out of your cerebral lockdown like your
outlaw sister might,
had you been nabbed by the sheriff for public wishful thinking.

You never want it to end,
but you know there are versions
and there are cover versions
and she is a world where there ain't no caves and there weren't
no Platos,
and Socratic debate is an infinite lunch break watching
episodes of Task Master to help the manna go down.
Easy like.
So you leave all the other people's parties before things get too
messy
and the stone star folds in on itself

and all our new friends become constellations of their own
as Jo (například) and I (for example) paint chess moves in the
midnight air of Stromovka park
connecting the dots of our beautiful, high, shining muses,
and remember it the way we always wanted it.

Cartomancer.
Belly dancer.
A new soul slow dials Dáme Romance.
Unnumerable friend comes with soft, white, Winter scarf
and detachable pro-nouns.
No add-ons necessary.

Wonderdust in 25-carat-gold beer contusions.
Hand-to-mouth combat in Happy Socks.
She-wolf snoozing in an Autumn arboretum. Her bark sweeter
than her sap.

Do not make her tell you twice.
I bought her a rice cooker so she could cook rice.

Practise what you preach and you can't go wrong.
Unless what you preach
is stupid!

CRIMES this feels good! I want to rename e v e r y t h I n g.

THIRTY-SIX

My window of opportunity open
just long enough to let in some fresh Apollinaire.
And if you pass by,
along the hill of Lumírova street
at just the right time of day,
in just the right season,
there you might see us,
wrestling on a wine bottle bed of nails
grinning at our pages that,
in our shy condition,
act as alternatives
to physical stages.

Two degrees of separation from Nabokov, Lennon and Pound
as I hand over Levy's change for his overpriced second-hands
from Prague's nouveaux underground
at which I man the helm and choose the morning muzak,

"Jazz, Michael. Jazzzzz..." Scott coos as he arrives,
book-alive,
first thing.

In Libris, Veritas: in Kava Vita;
in praní prádla.
And Kavárna Velryba cumulates us all
with one overheard conversation
and a lick of forest green paint'n'short shorts.

Mark, Maura, Marketa, Scott and Jasper,
I thank you from the bottom of my coffee fee fi fo fum-stained
heart.

The Prognosis the prognosis.
The Prague Post, post gnosis.

Forgive me my ungrateful and ill-mannered selfish,
and think of me more fondly now.
This dickhead semi-reformed thanks to a knock-kneed
nostalgia for your generous, Globular gifts.

A scouser in a Spaghetti Western –
outofplace, intheway, unbeckoned,
unreckoned and tolerated
till some bug-eyed Billy takes it upon himself to shoot me in the mouth
and put pay to my presence.
A bleeding heart.
No more prayer.

I raise my hand to ask Julian Barnes a question
only for Julian to be ushered out before he has time to answer.
Time up!
Beckoned to his holy typewriter
and no real sense of an ending.

A bleeding heart.
No more say.

Sean and Dave and I counting on the leftover Derby delivery
daytime sandwiches Ian toted from office block to office block,
and one day he didn't come home
and we role-played the phone call to his Mum
and her dropping the phone to the floor,
and the muted, muffled cries.
And he showed up two days later and went to work
and Sean and Dave and I counted on the sandwiches
and didn't have to call Mrs McCulloch.

THIRTY-SEVEN

A bleeding heart.
No more pay.
An underscored overdraft and pocket Penguin 60s.

Oxana bargains with the bards in triplicate.
Fuck you! Fuck you! And fuck you!
Banksy is Oksyi in a Yaxi Taxi.
As she plays, she kicks up a flurry of skinny ass micromanagers beneath her giantess pumps.
Wee little perverts trying to look up her dress,
and she stomps them out with that toothy smirk she reserves for the gibbons
who leave spittle on her plectrums and make lairs inside her guitar case.
Keeps her thoughts in a sequinned holster
by her side;
quick on the draw – deadly lemon – bitter priestess – singer songwriter.

I'll give you ten more minutes then I'm calling the cops.

Outspeaking the outspoken at the poetry slams she slams.
Wine culpable.
Text maniac.
Tertiary rattlesneak.
Pulmonary hufflepuff.
Emeralding her moods in multilayered power frets.
Analysing sound as it agonises over where it wishes to take her this time.

Music the only dominant above painting and literature.
Literature the only dominant.

Painting the dominant.
Beneath cinema and alcohol.

I project myself into one of those glistening cars down there.
The ones passing Podolí.
Away from this moment.
That look in her eyes.
A clamp on her long shot.

Alcohol above cinema, and literature a close third,
then music then painting,
not necessarily in that order.
But what does it matter?
Each day new personal restrictions.

That piercing glance gooey with disappointment
and disdain.
Disdain is the true dominant;
ain't no coming back from a look like that.
I don't care who you got playing on your headphones.
It's Oksyi?! Oksyi's on Spotify?
Well good for her. Let me listen...let me listen. Yes, yeah, music IS dominant.
Music cancels out the rest.
You know what would go well with this?
A cold beer and a book. Fuck your look.
A song, a beer, a painting, cinema and a book.
I weave and I dodge as you swing for my ego
and I 'man up' behind refreshments and poetry
and you connect every now and then
and it brings tears to my eyes
but I'm not in pain I just, I just,
I miss it when we used to hold hands and talk about the weather
and the Vyšehrad dead.
Nothing melancholy about Autumn leaves falling
and I barely remember your smile.

We have been at this for millennia.
You wrote like there was a secret. This is your mistake.
Two shots of bourbon please.

Heaven's Door!
Your body is your body and there's no such thing as temples or metaphors.
But...
you were special.

THIRTY-EIGHT

A toast –
To saying the same thing again and again and again.

If we could never die
there might just be a point to saying the same thing over and over again.
There's something we have not been telling each other.
And not cos we're shy,
and not cos we're coy,
and not cos we're tired.
It's because the words we have to use are the same and it's embarrassing. I
don't want my words to look like yours.
And I know for goddamn sure you don't want your words to look like mine.
So we juggle and conjure and squirm in existent fantasy.
Road movie suicides looped to margarita eternity boobs.
Fucking when everyone is looking,
and trying not to cum too soon for the show of it.

I kept having these really white feet.
Beautiful and scared.
I love you and you smell so good.
I'm a fucking suicide bitch with a pickup truck.
Czech cornflakes are too hard. Give me a leg up.
I'm one scrambled egg away from perfection.

We see through each other.
We know that the writers we love say what we think better than we have yet thought to say it ourselves.
We...are...one.
I, a red,

and your blow-up dolls are not welcome in my house.
I gathered up all the spit in my mouth and accidentally spat it
out on my carpet. Nothing lasts forever.
And there's some songs I would share in a mood like this
and sometimes forget
but would dream...one day...
I will karaoke this to your hearts.
Are you ready to come yet?

Lie down, December.
I love you too.
Now only play songs we can all sing along to.
"There is nowhere you can hide. Always standing by your side.
If you come back let me know. I won't ever let you go."

I would swim the seas to ease your pain.
I would correct you when you say penguing,
or squreouwel, or joowelrererrr.

And we buried ours and the dead buried theirs.
And we fought about who should brush up the dust of the
studio because I wanted to brush up the dust of the studio.
So much dust.
You don't even know.
No more daydreams of flowers and cream and puppies for me
now.
My ship.
My home.
My armless debate.
Coward milked in circular disability-thinks.

"Don't pity me. Don't pity me. Don't pity me."

"Don't drink me."

And I break into tears as you turn your face away from the
parade I arranged just for you.
Past glories no good.
Timeless themed sun gods in search of a voice that is silent.
Someone to hold you too close and hurt you too deep and sit in

your chair and ruin your sleep.
Yes. That's all there is to it...
no?

I know you too well. I read you all. I seen your pictures. I love you all!
So I know, I know.
I don't believe. I know.

Blow out the candles, you prick.
Want something.
And I ask, "Why have you locked me in?"
And you ask, "Who on earth do you think 'I' am?"

One of my least favourite things is a party with other people.

I sit down on the orchestra lip upstage,
like Danny Kaye first time performing in England,
and I get up close in your judgemental fuckfaces
and get sweet as fucking fuck.

"Least favourite of all...
People who say, "That's a bit before my time.""

The way she walks towards you when she meets you,
when she looks like she spent a month preparing to look like that,
when she walks toward you to meet you
and then the philosopher's lost notes fall from her hip pockets
as she prepares to look like she walks
and meets your notes falling from the way she walks
when she looks towards you and philosophises about the fall.

Good Star.
What a feeling to be yours.
Good Star.
What a feelin'.
Along the faultline.

"Oh, oh, oh, would you shut up, mmaaaaan?"

Candy come along, candy come along come along.
Blinded by the bright lights.
I only wanted from you,
three little notes.

THIRTY-NINE

Prague is a convalescent home for struggling artists.
Castle turrets coated in lucky bird shit.
Money spiders infiltrating the rusty cranial cavities.

"Perhaps a job in a shop isn't such a bad idea after all."

The brainiacs don't overthink, they underfeel,
and that's where I come in.
SpongeBob SquarePants with a degree in blatant, 'out there',
thirst quenching, Homosexual Philosophy.
I love that you are friends with me,
my big, ancient, pink, idiot, man-child.
The scoop is, there won't be an actual civil war if the cunt is
voted in/out,
or snuffs it.
But there will be a street named after him where all morons go
to die as we restart our families and praise the silence
on La Rue de la Merde.

Enter Vít, Prague left.

Vít capitulates.
Vít combobulates.
Vít serves up a warm dish of vengeance which we leave to cool
overnacht
to commemorate the successes of past analogically,
theoretical, outrospective,
virtual collective victories recorded in utero for future algoholic
speculators to sift through at junctures salivatory.

A man points at a garden feature. A boy starves in a blue state.
The electoral college shut down in the pandemic for fear of

spreading no sense whatsoever.
The one size fits all glass slipper fooling 'em for a while
until Vít comes along with sound alternatives.
Sound alternatives.
Alternatives to sound.

Jo makes coffee.

The flow, the nonstop, the permadumb revolutions not revolutions at all,
but one constant 'ing'.
Painting and photography stupefying the bleeding obvious.
All women are ugly.
All men are ugly.
What other species could convince themselves that a bird shitting on your head is lucky?

I am a distracter so this is a good 'ing'.
The words us Dodos share won't get us anywhere,
until we learn to undo grammar like a lion doesn't.

Listen to the trees. Those useless trees.
Vít KNOWS.

WE ARE ALL DICTATORS AT HEART
WE ARE ALL FOLLOWERS AT HEART

Let's go for a walk. Yes, bring your coffee.
We'll walk side by side and march this way for Neutral Extremism.
One profound, almighty 'NE!"
as you nurse that chilly beverage into the setting sun.

"I think this is the beginning of an extreme case of friendship."

FORTY

Chris and Stephen skirmishing tactics
across a bullet casing carpet in laureate attire
piled to the breaches with sentiment and atrocities, calumny
and hypnotism and a tank full of reindeer.
The calumny from the gym, and the reindeer to confuse the
masses.
But tough.
The battle ground egregious,
lolling to the communists' left
but pitted pattering on the precipice of the flat world about to
warp if it doesn't get the punctuation just so;
the pronunciation just so.

Stalwarts' victory wreathes made of sugar and honey and
marmalade grannies from back in the day when a cup of tea put
hair on your chest and deeper voices stuffed basins with fairies.

The cool, hard, cold, hard peace.
Crawford fights. Takes precedence over the Beastie Boys Story
with as many tragic nuances underwritten.
Delbos' name on the open mic readers list.
The subtle mechanics of a Scottish joker reeling in the middle
of his own passion play.
Tommy Dorsey ushers Frank in from another book and we
crane our heads to take a look
then continue.

'The Gathering of the Clans'.

Chris reads 'Battle'.

Christmas rears its subcutaneous head over Halloween
murmurations Mums imagine in their Sunday bests and arms
full of promises.

I promise you I will never die.
I promise I will live forever.

Youse going to have to lean in hard on those poems and poets
of yours till this pusillanimous virus gets sucked up into a
Stankovianska/Vichnar translation-hallucination of Phillipe
Sollers
committing heresy on the back of a 17 tram,
slappedandpassedaround
from yokel to yokel in the guise of a ragtag unhumblebum
(to the mellifluous strains of 'It's a Lovely Day, Tomorrow')
screaming,

'I speak six languages, fatass! Go jogging! Talking shit to me.
I can hear shit when you all talk. I can't breathe. I have a cold.
No, I won't wear a mask.
Go ahead call the police, you fatass!
Go for a run, you ugly Czech fatass.
I speak Czech better than you. Speak English for christ's sake.
I will eat too! Here on the tram.
What do you think of that?
Salmon. Right here in your faces.
None of you are two metres.
Why should I wear a fucking mask, you shitty fatasses?!'

Pen drops to floor.
Drug wares off and dreamstops.
Chris comes out from behind the snowman he made with
wrenches,
when he was just a nipper,
and he's alone now, and he's holding his stomach,
the laughter is hurting so good.
And he laughs until all the divinities in their rumpled nighties
sneak out of their dormitories to have a look at what earthlings
can do when they really put their mind to it.

Chris' poetry punches.
And it caresses.
And it skips all the ill notes 'cause it's pared down to the raw necessity of speech
in 'only words which matter'
and it matters and I go at mine with a fucking machete like Ezra Pound to The Waste Land
and I scrounge through the field of shallow graves
and scooping up the bullet casings for souvenirs I see stems sprouting from the ears and mouths of the fallen
and another tear comes to my eye
and I thank Chris for the loan of his wrench
and Google Delbos for the bang-bang of a different drum
and someone who could have been a comrade had the war not torn him from the local presses
and drafted him to foreign climes
to fight other people's wars for them.

FORTY-ONE

9:47 am

I found there was more to say when saying it wasn't so important.
And what's to become of this love of ours if we can't word it.
Croon it.
Something to remember us by. When one of us goes bye-bye.
I need coffee, eggs and a translator for these Egyptian Tarot.

What binds us all together is the beautiful, fucking weather.
Repeat ad nauseam. Now upload.

1370
Late medieval.

A third of us 'Europeans' deaded by dreaded Ploog
but then papered by the Chinese
for the love of Mamluk.
And I've gone and left my football boots at home and the keys to my home in the school.
You are losing patience and we're going to miss the glass blowing workshop at this rate,
Ploog or no Ploog.
Pips or no pips:
Variegated meme horses carrying us through the attrition.
1462. ANO to card sharps and trick-taking, for example.
And tumultuous straddling ensues.

And for the Little Story of the Universe I opt for a T.S. Eliot refrain coagulating Daddy issues and Tarology.
One birth is all it takes.

And thinner thinly copied and pasted;
as we start to look weaker the more we get wasted.

Notes and dates to memorise:

Visconti – Sforze: side saddles, ladies embossed and eagles of black, bloody love.
1650 Jean Noblet

1760 Nicolas Conver en Camoin

1782 Court de Gebelin's multi primitive world, volume eight. Twenty-two correspondences and Tetragrammaton collaborations.
Egyptian ties.
Ancient book of Thoth.
Worldly wisdoms preserved to a universal alphabet.
A clueless savant. The secret knowledge of a Freemason.

Enter Etielle.
The moment divination is propagated and read-read jam Solomon,
King of the mysteries shadowed through occultism's Shadrak.

Eliphas Levi who but for his cock would sainted be had boondocks.
Illustrated Satan and the roast is history.
Rectified the Tarot mid nineteenth, cuntury-cums all over the Foxy Sisters
three for one and Blavatsky!

1887 An esoteric order deciphered,
a cryptic, elusive foetus eaten in doodled sources.

The Hermetic Brotherhood of the Golden Dawn is born astride a yawning grave. Yeats is sworn, Waite is torn, Crowley is hung and drawn.

The Cards have totems become.
Pen pals with your devils and all your abstract gods.

1909 – Art' goes some ways to explicating the Hermetic secrets publicated,
Sola Busca-inspired,
and for nine months Pixie shudders and pulps a conjuring baby,
colourful tables of lamniscate Levi.

Crowley's diligence soaked and spilled in semen droplets smoothed out over many many years of Harris' monumuffled bomb letters.
Back to Egypt.
Pragmatic Yod Yod Jodo.
And repeat.

Petr Kohout is Pierre de Lasenic.
Name changed
because it just sounds cooler.

Marko and Jaro and Tyko and Jo and Asgeir and Willy and I taking turns at the wheel. Reading poetry from the backs of our baseball mits.
Beer-soaked bench warmers cheering us on,

"Go, man, go! Read us another one!"

Rare and beautiful. Sentient jocks. Character based poster children for the unpronounceable revolutiosnjksdjbjkwjdnejdajjaksjkjnckadjc.

"We'll do the show right here!"
As soon as the state of emergency wears itself thinly.

History designed inside out.
Us Magnanimous Seven are here to put pay to the notion that tugging on a thread will unravel Bog's underpants.
Would benefit us all to not have been unravelled!
"Genitals ahoy!"
Never mind worshipping the sun and the trees,
what about this junk we all have one foot above the knees?

And we have the Fool with the stoned insouciance only a family man can master,
and the High Priest younger than his art and whipping it like a good anarchist,
and the Trickster bombing the red tape into submission like a naked grenade-ninja, and Mother Nature holding all the cards but showing none till the time is right,
and Jesse James has been resurrected so she's got someone good to play poker with, and the Kangaroo cuddling his notes to his playmobile gestures lulling us all bravely into dreams of childhood-covered mountains,
and the Philosopher Clown grading the world like a long-legged head mistress in the skin of a scorned juvenile delinquent got the keys to the school reports,
and the Drowned Phoenician Sailor with his eyes fixed on the horizon despite the squidgy sounds of his confident, tentative, confident, tentative steep steps.

And more streets than rivers.
Always more streets in the good books.

Not Liffey lubrication or waters of Leith or River Dee dew or humbly Hudson drool, but Vltavská unguents joining our collective egos till we are all drinking from the same Small, Lennie jug
and falling down Karlova to Liliová
to memorials of undiluted Beef Stew in Jazz cellar armpits of ignorant Bethlehem. Capsulating Konviktská with lub –
from Ruská to Jana Želivského cradling other people's stories in my arms
like spasmodic fish-twitching-muscles
longing for the sea.

FORTY-TWO

An ill wind blows. I dropped my purse. He held my hand.
The Winter won't be the same.
Amputated Father. And hand.
Irresistible Český Krumlov.
Blood ties to Armageddon.
Louise Beer. Iva Nesvadbová, Andy Allen and a consultant
hung in a new tuxedo, calls himself sweety pie.
All connections present.
Gambit Gallery. Art Praguers. Prague Art Works. Hat tilting
anathema.
Asphyxia on the horn.
Marcus Aurelius mediates between the divorce lawyers we
forgot to hire, and I walk away with my dick in my hand and an
empty bank account;
a pauper, a pirate, a clown and a poet...

......walk into a bar...

That's life in The Big Rohlík.

You wire them up like a yuge collage Christmas parcel.
Chemistry gallery. Talking fast.
All alone. Shy. Skulking.
Electronic elevator muzak. Pulled up. Big smile.
Give us a wave. Say hello. Go on. Don't be a pugilist.
Move over gentle and dodge those sniper bullets and 'scuse you
while I disappear.
Youthful Hájek peripheries grooving on thesbyitis.
Helms and Hempstead homies.
Cold cuts, and you pay for the wine, to the vexation of the
Pigeon Fleet who rely on the free waters which come from the
street.

And I plow into your Elysian fields like a rusty bronze spoon
dragged along the neck of works in progress.
A chemical profile tonic.
A comical blind-sided permanent resident beats Bubenská jeden,
was when home of the paternoster crab nebulae,
and Ms Serran's first veryown go-atom atelier.
Umělec magazine snook and tidy,
post pretentious calamity jejunes.
Half-crazy Mečl and his Merry Chriticalmass combobulating
bookshelf messiahs in secular beer trappists' woolly stockings
torn off by a sprightly Ivan Mládek,
box-headed migrant-shunts kickstarted into play
instagrammatically incorrect
from Cyranův Ostrov and a scene stealing walk on from X.

The who-is-politically-incorrecter translating pow wows over
croissants and fruit bowls delivered in abundant refresh for a
national treasure and us subliminal entourage.
Jožin z bažin sharing hotels and gallery space in Olomoucian swamps,
done up special like.
Politician cradles from gallery owner TV huggers.
Right wing snugger buggers.

"The Prague Spring a foregone conclusion. The communists
were ready to hand over power even before the students took to
the streets."

The surface sighs shallow plenitudes within walking distance of
one deeper thought at a time.
His naive-art pictorial sing-alongs demand no unwrapping,
and mine would leave you alone too if you happen to be of a
perpendicular mind.
We comfortably reminisce in local plenipotentiary of foreign
comedy imports of import.
Ivo proffers George Formby, Little Britain and Monty Python.
I am aware of the village inhabitants' eyelines and frothy
adoration for my drinking companion.
"You get tired of the eyes all the time. It's the price we pay."

Loquacious, gentleman, Mrázek, mooks me at ease and
anglophones my awkwoddities.

Now the age of Horus implores us,
"Do not fight that same fight. Yours is of another dimension.
They unpaved the way for you. Smashed their drills and admonitions,
now you are free to do it yerself.
Your idols are dead. They cannot rebuke you for browsing on a different website. They know not what a website is.
It is up to you to fuck up your descendants.
You and you alone.
Be playful with this freedom.
Try and recall an idol who 'bored' you into liking them."

And so I turn to my dead idols as the High Plains Drifter floats by on a Prague-Boats-4 Hire boat.
"Well glue me to Fagin's bedroom window!"
he exclaims,
"Never borrow the gun you steal.
That tight feeling on the tram, under the mask, in your chest…
That's Coronoia, boy."

FORTY-THREE

With our belly-loads of convention we mutilated serendipitous invention-tykes
on barbed bicycle meep meep.
Elongated Tarmac hikes through rotting luxury apartments
only three weeks on the market.
Yacht stolen.
Bravura complex.
Get yer head round that, Mother.

'Oops,' it says, 'something went wrong.'

Truncated CEIs dancing and WOOTing to The Murder
Capitol at the Underdog's Ballroom.
The Milky Bars on Dan.
Music we had only ever seen the social screen written suburbs of.
Fuck first. Think later.

The credulous coddling of Krištof Kintera
and two coquettish sparrows;
one a Plutonian vulture couple,
and three the latent Midnight Child private vacation,
first class seat, missed opportunity, mother of intention.

We and will am love those bands.
We am will do see those groups.
ShitKid, Cherry Pickles, Twisted Rod,
and you get this picture in your head of Lou Reed and Julian
Schnabel and Laurie Anderson and Andy and Jean,
and I do my first sincere Crowlian reading
and it tells me painting is futile.
Certainly not worth catching Covid over.

As for 'writing',
it tells me of extreme happiness,
a lap of luxury, and active, never ending, adventurous love.
And Lou and Laurie and Julian and Asa Soderquist and Lina
Molarin Ericsson and Priscilla B and Mimi B 'Like' me as I spill,
having been badly positioned on the edge of the table,
into a better place,
onto better ground.

MothsandDemons, is this okay?
Is this okay?
Street strokes, spinning passionate,
whooping degenerate, gladly mammalian.
Christian Dadway.
I got the Emperor today and I felt ashamed.
I screamed at the gig. I told James McGovern to return. My
friends told me I love James McGovern.

Invention-tykes.
This is I.T.
A bottle of champagne for my Tesco trouble and accusations of
favouritism.
Bontonland;
my Černabilly imaginarium where you have what it takes and
make no mistakes and study Hip Hop, Sit-Coms, Cartoons and
Fiesta as a matter of life or death.
No cold last hope but bottomless pockets of love and lollipops,
cool herb,
Kool Herc
and bitchin' badges of all your favourite loud wet dreams.
MNFSTO bedroom-art turning me on!

Bontonland rainbow kissing Park Hvězda
where the columns of memory-gambits branch off into fragile
candelabras of green&attached love.
Loafing inanout the geraniums and planoutlouds.
Nobody near but the chicanery pragmatazoids and goosy
childrains all parented and Offsted.
Ice Cream beers and a break from one's fear of
underachievement.

I will learn how to make my own Zelňačka s klobásou one of
these days and then they will see!
They will alllll see!

I count on you to count me out
and leave me to my own devices,
striding to your guiltless towers
and tribal lawn-breached leisure stables.

Gentrified and clotted like the cream of a thousand dandroids,
clipped but for their webbing, seeded Tudor-like and swanky,
and I can't help wishing I had been there for the profiteroles
and spankings.
Still the rock cakes mutate aptly for a reaching cafe sprat such
as I;
pen drawn,
notepad bristling,
whiskers pawing at the waiters and waitresses.
Customers and miscellaneous inking their way into my
privatepublic yawpings.

Two beers for the Heresy,
three beers for the nouveau arrondissement,
four to take me home,
a melancholy gypsy boy caravanned and gladderly tanning the
hides of sultry ladies having trouble choosing where to sit.
"If there's one thing I have learned in life,
it is that ladies have trouble choosing where to sit."

We ain't no savages.
We is Sleaford Mods after the storm,
missing the stickiness of being organazised.
Rebel Without a Pause on a legendary graffiti documentary
like molasses nostalgia in pen-stripe zoot suits at a gangster
beat poet's fancy dress Valentine's Day massacre.
Oh the drama.
Oh oh oh the dramaturge.
Oh oh the writer
and the wisdom to know the difference.

FORTY-FOUR

Leaving weeded brains and acid balls on the carpet
of Mark Divo's living room floor,
returning hot returns.
Mrs Zlo's psychedelic, dark-taxes and pip pip hoorays.
Collaged collating,
Markéta Gariaeing ways into the psychomagic of our nový red
Ginsbergs and Gallery Gambit businesserry.
Their beautiful witchery,
academy-paddled park side rhymery.
Nursing Los Angeles peep shows more powerful than
knowledge.

Don't be a silly Billy, listen to the girls for deep deep hope
and the concept of conceptualism planted inverbally.
Domicile anger-tropes sprayed up the walls of your crumbling
academy halls,
ripped from the chests of tired, old D.J.s.
Your mansion eyes and gargoyle Freemasons cemented to your
back yard smokers' stained overalls and pitches.
Stromovka herding the anal coffee mooks
and selling flashbacks of derelict picnics carved into fences
and something in your poems.

The Devil / The Aeon / The Hanging Man
The artists' perennial finance plan.

And a Hopkirk, skip and a jump away,
Tereza Silon needs cashes for a lemon-glazed honeymoon,
reads from Kabbalism's free basing cold crush in Beseder.
And Randall's played by Jim Moir but we never had a telly
and less is the pity.
Besides, Tereza nails it with a toothy smile and a fully clothed

charm-bomb,
feet up,
Cinzano Bianco memory exmachinas.
Czech bandstand in tit-biting world appeal,
living room downsound approved by the queen of swords,
gritty realcheeks,
kick it kick it, wrap it in a dishcloth,
mucus-gilfed and rubbed into Cross club's tight panty brain cells.

She's nubile colloquium and spiritual menagerie,
gob-brazen-angel-carer,
maple-flavoured bacon sheen.
One distraction after another. Like a peddler at a state asylum I wear my wares and pray for a more successful round of electro-therapy.
I throw in my chips and bet on an illustration of an illustration of a positive schizophrenic.

What I need is an operating room that doesn't fall apart before our venerable Venables gets the chance to coax French into me by ways of a servant woefully ignored.
I mean it's a classic.
They thought different back then.
White classic.
Can't blame them for that.
Can you blame them for that?
Oh you can!

Eco-logicals.

There's strength in Black and White;
a rotting, beautiful imbalance in colour.
It's bad if the candle burns but doesn't drool.

Doesn't every young man have an obsession with St Sebastian?
That aloof expression as the umpteenth arrow tickles his existence.
Oops, something has gone wrong!

Yup, here comes the fortune teller's heart attack.
TRINC!

I mean where did love ever get you? How's that been working for you?
Another tactic. Another poem. Another suburb.

TRINC!

The Ace of cups / The Empress / The Aeon
The artists' faith in the power of Psion.

I'll print it large and put it on my wall.
It will 'mean' something to me. I will 'get it'.
How pleased I shall make myself.
Adjusting the ego sentence by sentence, image by image.
Feeding...feeding...hungrier and hungrier and hungrier.

It's a heavy table.
Never mind the beggars.
This table can take the weight,
and that very specific aroma a baseball develops. Sweet sport.
Babe Ruth pierced.
Aloof.
The indescribably perfect unnameable perfume of a story
quotidian, rising to peregrine heights.
The Fitzgerald of a diary.
Maya Deren holding hands with an ensemble cast of overpaid actors paying the overdue rent for a brown skinned Utopia.

We'd all rather be Tony Montana than Charles Bukowski anyway.
And we each create our own room.
Tutankhamen's tomb.
The Magician in night fever.
High high high.

Besides

Besides, the game 'Catch' ain't about catching as much as it's

about throwing.
To toss that leather hard as you can an' not lose the ball.
That's what it's about, man.
That's the be all and end all.

Colostomy Gangsta Rappers keeping it reel.
Mrs Evil & Miss Garai & Zuzana Žabková conducting
demonallergies through bright yellow, intellectual vaginas
caught on film in drizzly phone videos discovered at the bottom
of a turgid, orange ocean of early morning blood debates.
Neck and neck and neck in fistivul cracker jokes,
pulverising the patriarchy in off-colour barbs and jibes
and kneel down
and pray you don't get branded by these sick sweet Sunday
blasphumers.

You ain't talking your way out of a tattoo like they!

Documenting the universe in ritualistic shit bags and 'Make
up for Dummies', clarifying God-Not-God and wild man Mike
bathed mild.
We ain't yelling, we ain't fighting,
we is working, dude.
Were KING!

Zuzana at the decks, launched like a luxurious beat on the floor
of the Meet Factory. She tha reverse of police brutality.
She tha stoned parental guidance of an affiliated tree hugger in
spiky ass britches, horny, thorny and black as NUI,
the goddess in Thelema.

FORTY-FIVE

Rounding the turretless, a second lap
thinking when-might-was the last time has-maybe-been
an English man and a French woman united
over Baseball in the Czech Republic?

Everything is changing.
Všechno je jiné.
There can be no return. Nemůže být návratu.
A shift in moral, practical consciousness and boxer shorts.
Use the liquid cleaners if you want, but just a cap full.
Ban alcohol and there will be a revolution.

Nosferatu Saves!

"My worst fear is that she thinks me shallow because I love
everything. I don't love everything. It's hate that drives me. Hate
that it is not love that drives me. Hate of what they have done to
me. Hate of what I allow them to do to me.
Hate of all war, religious institutions,
poverty
and friends who insist on telling me how slow my computer is."

I do not love everything. I do (not) see a lot (a lot) to (out there)
love (fantasise) out there (in) though.
And one of the sincerest forms of struggle for positive change I
know
is poetry.

Of all the arts,
it is poetry that promises the smallest possible financial gain
and the least possible chance of achieving fame.
But, order a Poet to put down their pen,

and they will write a fucking poem about it.
The answer is there for the taking...

"Stačí?"
"Nestačí! Stačí, ne!"
"Proč?"

Because you think you have an answer you can share.
You cannot share that which is not passed through liquid.
The ever-lovin' cap full.
The most influential of you only ever scratched the surface.

"Thiz we know. Thiz we know. Thiz...we...know."

The louder we cry about 'people' not doing enough,
and how little we do ourself,
the louder the beasts of the Bible become as they beat their
chests and laugh at the sun into which they cum.
Now satiated.
Still begging for an invite to the party.

Oh what I wouldn't give for you all to admit to wasting the day
carving soap operas into gubs and relishing the reference.

FORTY-SIX

Overture Overdue.

I skipped the news and fake-made-plans-with-you.
An' now I'm lettin' ya go.
This the Atu X.

This the unwanted, expected mantra of Bloomsburied Gropers everywhere.
Play to your limitations.
And if you are very very good,
we will let you mix yourself a screwdriver and enjoy the accomplishments of those who outreach you.
One can join High Society easy enough,
but to be yourself while you are there,
that is the key,
and the key crossing that key, and the minor key, the major key
and the person you always wished you would be.
The one you met on your Mother's knee.
And you Gotta look.
You don't Gotta look hard but you still gotta look,
cos there's folks out there who are so themselves they can
leave you with an ache in your stomach the shape of a vinegary conker,
pricked,
played with,
and leaving you puzzled by the fact of them.

Huckleberry Finnegans woke late,
stunted by our screechy, drunken finishing school.
Rummaging in the roots.
Scrabbling on my hands and elbows in search of things lost.
Would you trade places with yourself?

Note: Jupiter's secret lies in the contradictions. The paradoxes. The tremulous inconsistencies. The true love.

My castle walls holding me alone to the task of reading the inscriptions on these mossy tombs.
My heart is ready to be re-patroned.
The horse chestnuts rolled and repositioned.
A spade and a heart. Aces I presume.
The canvas once again blank for the heart and the intellect.
A Gothic sklep from here to maternity.
One more exposition and a free ticket to the dungeon I have kept locked all this time.
Chronos, egg-shaking-impatient,
god-making-indulgent,
fridge magnet simplicity
of the infinite bound.

"Awwwwww,
his first words...."
We are united, us buried.
Hostages to hysterical laughter. A hostage to hysterics.
Can't keep pretending.
And you can't say goodbye to books.
Can't keep pretending.
You can't say goodbye to books.
The paradoxes. The tremulous inconsistencies. True love.

"We are our conversations," she said.
I think the same thing, I said.
And she thought the same thing.

We...
We ARE already.
Universal solipsism underexposed in the musty twilight of belief in others' otherness.
Undamning redintegration.
The eternal return to who and what we are.

"You don't need our help. You had the power to go home all along."

I know it's not the teachers' fault.
They have been taught from the start that there are things
which need to be taught in order to be paid.
Known knowns and deliberated abstractions;
carefully planned surrealities;
the manufactured unconscious.

You are an obstruction.
You are my only hope.

And God knows we love to complain.
And so Becket works,
against all odds.

We
Are
Lucky.
Quaquaquaquaquaquaqua
Plus one Canuck.

And Eliot dug Chandler and Groucho and peaches.
And farting makes us laugh even though we are all here,
and from gas we came
and to gas we are delivered,
not with a whimper but with a chuckle.

And oh but the weight of comedy.
Around and around, and on and on.

From the same dream a thousand years ago.

'The answer to your question has already been revealed.'

FORTY-SEVEN

In this room there rests the answer. Shelved.
In this Lumírova apartment oasis.
Nusle nestling numerology.

INRI IAO LUX
The light.
From right to left. From bottom to top.
On!

Meet The Beatles – Star Special – Number twelve – Two and Six
Death Crap M*A*S*H MAD No.234
Star Trek hidden NCC – 1701
Superman No.1
Penguin Modern Poets 10
POP!
Man and his Symbols – 5 essays
Harpo Speaks – Harpocrates/Groucho/Rowland
The Marquis Went Out at Five – Draft 333
A Superman egg cup filled with four leaved clovers if it's not too much to ask.
Misery dancing.
The American Magazine – The Finer Points of Baseball
10cents. Same price as issue one of Superman.
All in full colour.
Terry Cashman's Talkin' Baseball – 12 tracks
Fonzie's Favourites hidden. Sit On It.
Tier 2. Frame 1.

Lucky is Alienist issue VIII
Conker conker, helicopter, Bila badge on eternal green curtain belt and Saturday Night Live – Album the First

The skull the skull the skull the hat!
The Fantasy Book from Dracula to Tolkien 1978
Dalek – Red
Finnegan's Wake 1992
3 casino chips
Liverpool Plectrum L25
Performance – Certificate 18
Marcus Aurelius – Meditations – Penguin 60s – chopped – cheap – nice
Word Addict – final edition – full – gone
Vic Reeves 'Big Night In' annual 1991
Third tier, pit stop' red wine, shut down.

Don't know if I'm happy, but I do think I'm in heaven.

Tier three
The Groucho Letters – Eliot's weight
The Graduate – Mrs Robinson's leg
Silent Screen – Spring Books 1973
The Maltese Falcon – Dashiell Hammett 35 cents in 1961
Two Virgins – rude – not that rude – no, yeah, very rude.
OH, THE PLACES YOU'LL GO

Tier one. Frame 2.
Lauren and Alice Edgar, happy birthday uncle fuzzy head
Maroon Beanie Xmas gift from California Chants
Merde d'artiste No.38 with conker.
Born Standing Up 1988 topped off with a bunch of Stone Roses
And the Microcosm Macrocosm mini–Beatles lunch box tin
Gill got wrong right
Watchmen graphic novel, Rebel Without a Cause DVD
Another Word Addict, without me in it and the Larousse Encyclopaedia of Renaissance and Baroque Art with all of us in it.

Tear 2. Bottle 2. Emotional animal digging deeper into the earth in which, the stone will be discovered, the higher we go.
Hollywood Babylon II
3 Ace men on a boat
Violent Femmes and The Tempest

A now I am 6 badge
Two men and a little lady and oh, the Strangeness of Beauty
Classic Czech playing cards and an Anglesey shell
The Red Sox beat the Cardinals and Doris Day shot us all to hell
Kenneth Anger – Alice L Hutchison
Tarot Egypcio 1971
Ovid's Metamorphoses and Hollywood Babylon 1 too.

Tier 1
Don't tell me your dreams. Not because I suspect they are meaningless but because they booooooooore me so.
Blue Jays baseball cap, John Lennon's In His Own Write, Carrithers' City Primeval
And 52 Betty Paiges. Melchior, Vichnar's Second Through Brain translation and my sister's first home,
A ticket for a post lockdown walk in Průhonický Park over Raymond Queneau's Stories and Remarks
A war time pocketbook of the Rubajyat of Omar Khayyam and the best looking The Libertine by Louis Aragon you ever seen
The Lasenic Tarot and the wee bookie wook 'Tarantula' by Bob Dylan
And finally
top left
A pair of black binoculars.

Tiers run dry.

Time to count. Additup additup additup...
16446 – One plus six plus four plus four plus six
21 – two plus one
3
The Magic Number
Born 3pm on the 30th of the 3rd
Book 3 of 3
The Infinity Collection.

Now move on.

Can't go on.
And in walks the child.

FORTY-EIGHT

Crumbs in Medusa's lair.
You dropped 'em for me. Most aspects unique.
Most aspects firsts.
Most prospects an audience and performer combined then
split to a duality drunk from a philosophy insult-tube.
All ones and tens, frames summed two in three tiers
with four posts holding.
My bed.

The discs, the discs, the books, the discs,
the shit and boxes, hats and eyes.
The Hat. The Hat, I'm a member of that!

Titty Twisted Lazy Fuckers,
Black Sheep Jehovah Witnessing Space Man smoking Pop Star,
and the only man I ever spooned.
Jerry Among Us, my munti tamelted yoopster gone Dada.
A sugar spun armoury of Horo devices and cumulative vices
and sticky guitar picks
and incendiary licks.
Drinking in holes and tunnels and veins and lifting our dreams
above our heads so they could see better the baobab horizons
and red Madonnas.

Sanguine hopes spread out like a Private dick's living room
floor
covered in notes and photographs and scrap book clues,
and they know the answer is lying there right under their nose
but can't seem to get the picture of Elvis fucking the devil out
of their heads.

Proofness of a maybe slap.

You broke my head with your gift and I threw you under the tram.
Kept apart by a blue grass pandemic,
high as secretary birds sniffing all that glue.
In your garden trading hangover aces, in baggy swim swams
of an eight-metre circumference, eight-foot-deep paddling pool
of no consequences whatsoever.
A shoddy hiatus.
Intergalactic beetle bum, caterwauling synergy down the lost lanes
of a Zeman-voting sídliště.

Cast off.
We shall see-saw our own roots and fool's gold.
I ain't going nowhere.
See you on the dreamy side.
The United migration of the Fall.
Undamning redintegration.
Goddamn the resistance.

An end to this long and inky conflict. An end to allegory.
Speak for yourself.
Ask for Mat.
You'll find him in Vyšehrad. This place.
This place has goodgood energy.
Rosy Cross. Orphic Egg. French Toast.
I'm nobody.
Sidestep the redlight district and head straight for the park.

And it's tiring. Even with these six fingers.
Even with these six toes, it's hard to care when all those that do,
do so for veeeeeeery different reasons
and to veeeeeery different ends.
It's tiring.

Lies ain't what they used to be.

Deep breath...I Am Eight. Deep breath...I Am Eight.
I am the arcana of Strength.
I am the highest and the lowest.

I am the microcosm and the macrocosm and I have woken at 3am
and felt it, known it, seen it
and been it.
Both at the same time.
Like there's no 'both' but just the one fat thin big small tall short tiny large unnameable object that is a very-thing.

What is written by one cannot be understood the same by two.
Somewhere between a Meme and a Crowleyism
lies the t-shirt which shall bind us. Unbind us.
Put an end to the Oxymoronic temptation to ridicule logic
and maybe pump us up just enough to pull logic's tail from between its beastly legs and beastly make sense!

Poet – Sometimes when we try not to make sense we make sense.

Logician – sometimes when I try to explain to my wife why I said what I said in order to make her feel better I end up just making it worse,
but if I stay quiet and say nothing this often hurts my cause even further,
which is not fair because I honestly don't think I did anything wrong.

FORTY-NINE

From the second gate I take a left (one turning before the Bystro with a Y)
and with due forethought and reason I veer left again above the sunken tennis court
and invisible amphitheatre crowds munching hotdogs and holding ghost-hands in the stands.
Two degrees removed from Martina,
so three removed from Virginia and Chris,
so four removed from the Cliff to which I am approaching.

Mat is hereabouts,
'Mat! Mat! Maat!'

Try to spend as much time looking into people's homes as looking at the sky.
We tend to miss it in the city. Take it for granted.
I take a running jump at myself and miss.
I follow myself anyway in an attempt not to go completely insane
without her.

A heavy sigh
releasing a twenty-six-year-old face, snow-smushed sister recorded for Christmas posterities
and we laugh till we muted-cry.
And in the sky above me a drone stares its insufferable thousand-yard stare signifying the end of days and privacy and the pride which can be taken
in not becoming the owner of a drone.

The blonde river which stretches from November 20th to December the 8th

and ends with a translation of one into three
and a creamy sugar destiny.
The yacht club integrity.
Blackpool light thoroughfare.
Mediterranean glamour puss.
Žluté lázně Ferris wheel, a pencil, a pad, topless ladies and me,
scrying memories to see what we can see,
beside the seaside beside the sea.

Poet – I see a great city whose glory touches the stars.

Logician – I see a thousand pointy spires, rain clouds and brothels, sun blisters, markets, stale twixes, seventies carpets and curtains and new wine and lovers and plush offices filled with the beautiful and the dead, and more coffee shops than you could paint in four lifetimes specifically dedicated to painting coffee shops.

Hacking through the hubbub now with sensitivity and broken headphones,
kicking acorn missiles into the path
of close-talkers
and skipping the shitty songs that have gate crashed their way into my Spotify release radar because I still haven't blocked my ex from listening on her device.
Sidling towards the statuary
protected by mythological giantesses sporting breasts the size of obese men's' stomachs,
and giants with feet the size of perambulators for identical triplets.

Breathe the mystical energies. Seize the den.
Buy an ice cream and plan what then.
In my chair. In my bit of the park.

Certain days are not meant to be wasted. And so we stay sober, so that the next drunk will be that much richer.

There's warnings on Disney films now about the racism.

FIFTY

Havlíčkovy Sady,
a sponge of another landscape.
Related and reviewed for monthly screenwipes
depending on abode-abouts.
Mongering on when life was slow and we crammed lifelines into
welcomed and fed sun days.

And Neil was there and Craig was there and Rose and Tom and
Ina and Barbora and Jonathan and Jim and Mia and Johnny
(R.I.P.) and Gary and ZeeKat and Peter and Andrew and H.
And I scampered down the hill a ways
from the C.Monts birthday bamboo
and pictured it in a capture valve, modelled on Le Déjeuner sur
l'herbe
for melons and scriptures of coldening pivos.

And broke into the scene
at night in my studio
with Pikachu and Daniel Johnston and Captain America
and a Tonka truck destroying Trumps wall
and the Wicked Witch of the West
and Wild Poppies near Argenteuil in Hornbach oils and
mixtapes.
Wall is Over (if you paint it).
See-saw pink it.
Drop-kick the K.F.C. baby and don't look back.

I looked you in the eye here,
and the skin of the noon goosebumped at family ties,
when things were simpler if you just wheeled your sorrow into
the fence,
and whatever makes you happiest, dear.

Yes.
Yes, dear.
We were wed here.

Varietal Wine Mappery.
My little finger slips longer in my head to a full stop.
Typhon towers and Zelda's apartments,
Černý's melty car station policed by low expectations.
The Podolí swim shrinking my index finger,
crawling like that with hands clawed like eagles' talons
worrying the ring.

Daydreaming rowboat shopping along the milk chocolate banks
(but good chocolate)
a quarter mile from numbered days in a four-floor house
and unseen time tunnels drifting argument to argument in
Dívčí Hrady thin quilts.

The severe new mercy of a pickled compliment, sweet and vinegary.
A walk through a beautiful field full of landmines.
Monkey mind they call it.

And plus we got our place in shush shush,
with hearts in each other's hands all sharesies
and but then plus hand sanitisers for the earth inheritors losing
themselves within their own eyes.
The heating a happy accident of car repairists;
the forgotten, unsung artists of a bygone age
when men were cats
and Morrissey was yet to fuck up good.

Online red boudoir Tarot readings.
Wine for sanity.
Postponed dreams.
Videos botched together for virtual gallery mouth to mouth
and remember Beechums Powders?

Awwww, Beechums.

Above and Below the same when sung in glossolalial verbiage
hung on an oily social realist washing line
when bras were bras and a husband might look forward to all
tomorrow's panties.

"It's not like we never warned you," Lisa says.
With rage comes great responsibility, and so what if the tunnel
through the bedroom-mountain isn't really a tunnel but a
painted on one Wiley Coyote knocked out while you were busy
at work today?

"I'm not angry. I'm just disappointed. It's not like we forced you
to get a job located miles away from the bedroom," Lisa says,
bla bla bla.
"Now give us a kiss."

In the genial path of the Isolation Collection great strides
are being taken to emulate God's ten emanations in one fell
president.
No new liberal programme but a guesstimate of the length of
time it might take for fifty-something creatives to blow the lid
off this thing and state plain like, what it is.

What it is.

Room five is dark.
And Černý may not be the most famous David we have to
display.
Robert knows someone who performed on a song with Bowie.
Might have the Eno brothers on board too,
thanks to Bethany Jacobson,
and Bethany Jacobson thanks to Brian and Rog'.
...wait...no,
we don't have the Eno brothers onboard.

Fuck the Eno brothers.

FIFTY-ONE

Ai Weiwei leads me by the dinghy
to the cheeky occupation of a V.Ai.P. seat at the National
Technical Library,
one uncomfortable bench behind the crick reserved
for Brian Eno (N.O.B.)

And stationary galloping beside me, one of the future four
horsepeople
of an I.C. anti-apocalypticon.
Hagai, a learned minister of conceptual curatorials sez 'NO!' to
nonsense and uncorroborated authorials.
Give him a yes and a no,
a straight line and a goal;
a professional smile and a map to the show.
He'll cut through the carp with the carp's own bones
and pin the award on the magpies' new homes.
One for sorrow, two for joy,
the recipe evident by the look of the dish and thirty more
wishes for your final wish.

Karel Schwarzenberg sleeping off a millennia of feudalism and
a head full of well used, well deserved, soap opera boxes
on which he slammed human rights violations
and then took an open-eyed quick nap on judgement day,
which is every day,
and the machines turned against the human race and we didn't
mind so much, having gone Netflix-blind in all six eyes.
Sleep Karel, sleep well,
for you are one of the last remnants of the fairy tales which
made the Czech Republic what it is,
and you can stream them into your home now
like Chianti from the teat of a flesh-coloured funnel.

And when you wake, don't forget,
that's NOT a real tunnel.

So back so to the common regenerator of us all.
Fairness.
The Conan denominator. T
he pronoun eliminator.
Peace,
energetic traction,
and the nonchalant couldn'tgiveafuckness at not getting a reaction.

Self-perpetuating perpetual motion,

subsidised by the wheels of another's good fortune
to have been cast as Lucky's understudy in lieu of an actor of real substance abuse.
I'll wait till six to get my drinkies,
then watch Beckett to help me think.
And as a reward for being so patient
I'll eat like a pig and make myself pregnant.

Distraction our common progenitor and ooh,
I haven't been to the Botanical Gardens or Charles University in a while.

"When does the sun set?"
"6pm."
"Remember Spangles? And Texans? A man's gotta chew what a man's gotta chew."
"Be fair.
Stop thinking about thinking."

That'll do for today, pig.

Stop. Stop. Stop. Stop. Stop. Stop. Stop. Stop.

FIFTY-TWO

LGBTQs asking churches to be more welcoming.
African Americans asking the Ku Klux Klan to invite them to their barbecues.
Oh my god,
oh my lord,
oh my god,
oh my lord.

There are no famous avocados.
There are some lions in England.
There are horse chestnuts in my right-side jacket pocket I use as worry balls when Winter beckons.
She screams she says.
She pulls her hair forward over her face n' looking like the big purple people eater drums the new world symphony with her paws on the table from Eunika's balcony. Reads the crowd.
All eight Billion.

No notes to speak of.
All-inclusive ding ding.
Like the pretend joined up writing we both did as kids;
an unlikely pair of glossololigagging, graphomaniacs.

I done kissed you, baby,
now won't you do the Chicken Walk with me?

Chin-diapers on.
School's out.
Park's lively.
Dogs and Mums happying,
and busied Dads wondering in my face what it must be like to have nothing, absolutely nothing to do.

I wonder in a dad's face,
'What's it like to have a kid? Oh you have two I see...Three! You have three kids, ahhh, yes I see, coming round the bend on his little scooter. Two boys and a girl so. You ain't never gonna have 'nothing to do' ever again!'
And I see an old guy,
about my age,
alone with headphones, like me,
and hands in pockets doing his castle rounds, like me,
and I think 'how sad'.

I see a young woman,
about my age, with headphones,
walking alone, doing her fortress rounds, like me,
and I think, 'how nice'.

And then I remember what binds us.
The knowledge that one day the sun will engulf the planet in careless flame and delete
Every
Written
Painted
Printed
Rumoured
Idiot
Wasted
Living
Thing.

"Moo-Ma and Poo-Pa, I met someone. I want to sell paintings but it's going too slow. I'm going to the moon. I don't want a proper job.
This is the desk, and this is the chair.
Au Natural.
Now give me your attention!
Have a nap. Alter your accent. Better your attitude.
I had a very very bad day."

Marlowe-brusque, wordless illegal outdoor Djin and Miscatonics,
brown-bagged, actively unforcing my derivatives.
With cool, dark eyes
I held her gaze.
Her look seemed to say, 'Not in. Any message?' I had nothing.
I open an old book of pictures from Hollywood's silent movie era for inspiration. With a thin stick of charcoal I sketch out a picture of Hasil Adkins hunching over a recumbent Gloria Swanson.
She got the idea.
We reenacted the scene right there on the canvas.

Smudged.

Trantina swallowing the last dregs of Alchemy and Minstralism,
then spitting it all back up in a tight imitation of Hollywood's Babylonian watchwomen on all fours,
lashed and leaning in to better hear the whispers
of immortality glossy
and evident.

"Nothing is obscure," he says with a wide, toothy smile.
Teeth in his hair, in his shirt, in his fingers.
He scoops a tremendous amount of house paint from the skull of one of his heroes. Splats it on the linen tundra.
It glows.
It's messy.
It's titled.
"Nothing is obscure. Nothing is obscure," you hear the porn stars whisper.
The mucky magazines crumpled and glued onto the mountains.
Step back. It's a mountain. They are mountains.
You can see if you squint now that there's four mountains.
Two ladies,
elephants,
hens
and a sniffling bionic dog.

One hundred thousand first time gun owners registered this month
and each one of 'em stapled to the context
of this mischievous maestro's machinations.
The suicides,
the accidental shootings,
the domestic violence taken to evil, high conclusion.
Amerika pinned in satirical bile,
varnished and cum-covered for future archaeologists
to uncover with a squeal.

We make our own mess in paroxysms of coughing.
The Fool excavates our remains
and takes them to the King of Pentacles
who pays the Fool in the memory of coins
then hangs the poor bleeder by his ankles.

The Stuckists too successful.
Everyone becomes an artist.
With the Fool all tied up, common sense becomes unbearable,
taking itself for granted,
eating way too many hotdogs.
Nailing way too many heads on walls.
Everybody will be famous.

The decapitation manifesto – Every head on the wall tells a story.

FIFTY-THREE

Two animals as one.
Two childhood fears in one.
Balance dying to become balanced.
Evil kissed and drowned.

Sylvia Plath'n'Tom Hughes
Gertrude Stein'n'Alice B.Toklas
Humphrey Bogart'n'Lauren Bacall
Kenneth Anger'n'Anton Szandor LaVey
Henry Miller'n'Anais Nin
Gilbert'n'George
John Lennon'n'Yoko Ono
Richard Burton'n'Elizabeth Taylor
Robert Mapplethorpe'n'Patti Smith
Bob Dylan'n'Joan Baez
Jasper Johns'n'Robert Rauschenberg
Martin Luther King Jr.'n'Coretta Scott King
F.Scott Fitzgerald'n'Zelda Fitzgerald
Katherine Hepburn'n'Spencer Tracy
Tony'n'Cleo
Petr'n'Helena
Tyko'n'Sandra
Bert'n'Ernie
Sausage'n'Pickles
Nick'n'Nora
Sandy'n'Danny
Dick'n'Dora
Famous couples / Tight breast chasms / Brave tone jerkers / Helmet counterfeiters / Vanguardians of the Galaxy / Silly little adds for 'LOVE' / Morning stars / Silly little acts of 'PEACE' / Maple leaves of grass...class clowns...
something to be.

The Zombies have adapted, developed military style tactics;
communicate with each other now,
give themselves names,
share news in grunts;
a common idiocy resulting in the absolute impossibility of
effective leadership.
The Dark Web,
a chance for communal solitude,
the holy grail for sale,
no firewalls, no fences, no future or past tenses.

Bring back the black and the red and the lost fishnets of
meritocracy.

Whatever your allegiance, we's all on the Lewton Bus.
We got to choose to choose to get off that bus
and be quiet as Maus.
Let's stop scaring the bejesus out of our children.
Let's stay outside.
Let's hold hands.
Let's eat.

Then we loot.

There is an egg inside me which is bigger than my body.

Robert gathered his poodlefishes and PopRats
and photogened the Bremen Nacht.
The bad nights and the good nights
across the room from Berlin Nude, New York Hink and Prague
Spools.
In the shiny shadrack he memed,
'DON'T BERATE THE HYPE. DISCUSS.'

And you who golly lactate, zoom zoom your dilating pupils,
in Herschel retrograde unt sun-kissed bed
your memories of a university armoire.
Slayer on the transistor radio you keep tucked inside your
murderer's overalls
and ooh, you do smile pretty.

There's no way I'm losing you.
Golden Invaders, Black Showers.
Cassandra happening.
Blue moon water announcement
and all the news passed on in breathless regenerate
and quadrupled understatement.
Modest? I nearly paid his streaming fee!

They call it progress. I mean an innocent bit of flirting never killed anyone.
His hair like a...like a...liiiiiiike Louisiana rain.
His ribs older than his frame.
His clothing made of mountain.
Shoes of Gogo, tied right by Didi.
Ancient channelling mouthpiece,
forgetful marquis de la betterment of madkind.
He is the first fall of snow in camoflagellating combat booties
making up his mind whether it is righter to err in the face of
grammar done in cool pastels
or unterraform the planet earth like a big, new, invisible throw
to cover up the wine and blood.

Rap up his corpse in a yellow Lacoste cardigan
but be sure to keep one eye open when you sleep;
this renegade star man is going to rage against the dying of the
art of convolution, and
for dressing him like a tool,
exact dire retribution.

Where the self-imposed Porto guru lies,
with his harem of academy demoiselles d'Avignon
in a re-flux action home built by the Egyptians
falls catamite stencil whores from the scarlet battalion light shades
raining Germanic philosophies bottled in baby skin water bottle brown bags.

Drink it, don't think it.

Nautical neighbours swim swarming fastly at your fifth-floor

battlements
croaking under the weight of rebellious crownies declaring themselves
'Well up for it!'
The noise machines scattered in genius genial.
Make yourself at home – make yourself a home.
I dreamt of a Solution and the spires aspired.
I bought myself a kazoo and kazoomed.
I hired myself a maid and she breeded.
I sold a finger painting on a mascara-stained duvet,
which was no longer needed.

The money comes from cardinals lambasted in the brickwork,
made to shut up and rethink their lives.
The money comes from unpractised practises chalked on the floorboards,
smudged by pedestrians
heard the party through the dangling intercom.
"What you got up there? Who you got up there? What you got up there?"

In-studio deejay plays tasteful sonata, indie-rump toe tappers,
in girlish pyjamas.

Epicurean mud fights over who's gonna blow the host tonight.
Put coins in the tip jar and the acid in your sweet talk.
"Take a beer, help yourself, make the bed, let her in, let her in,
and her, and her, the more the merrier until you've had quite enough."

Yeahhhh, three nights.
Three nights is just about enough, till the next exhibition
conceives of itself and invites the contemporary girls and boys, ladies and gents
to this and other and similar events
where the self-impeached proto guru tickles the liveries
unlocking youth's potentials via lectures in bad housekeeping.

Humble and brilliant,
accomplished yet fresh,

as a gothic orgy scenario or smoky mnemonic tempest.
I remember ideas and sensations with pictorial reference aids if available.
S'why I collect all the magazines.
S'why I know all the best words.
S'why I take photographs when I am two sheets to the wind,
to surprise myself with forgotten events three days later when I wake all covered in paw prints, myself and your wicked coven's lipstick.

The music plays on in brain-sold thrum thrum – I can't believe it's not Flora.
It's all in the mind,
and body,
and cosmos.

Alors, je suis un Dada Freak. Ich bin eine iconoclast!
The tears flow free into my prescient cheeseburgers
and don't let up till Ruska street
when the sun shakes its shaggy wet coat all over my guilty hang ups.
The sounds of the world go in and out like when you're listening to Spotify on your phone and you get a message, but the message is muffled and misleading and you call home,
"It's alright Ma. It's alright Ma, I'm only bleeding. Ho ho."

Bob Dylan, Pavement, Yeah Yeah Yeahs, The Wedding Present, Public Image Limited, The Murder Capital, Twisted Rod...

Dayglo naturals, smoke machine amble-mods, cellophane gas masks, indoor cigarettes, offline atom-trams, photo bomb oracles, cocaine propane mouth jobs, backstage liptards, cool bean hair struts, late paying army buddies, brain fucking studio Martians, locked in remix Blooms, Shatterhand's Everest, no limit LOVE VOLE Fisher Price 'night club', fake mink germ cull celebrity taxed woke Viagra! Gamble TOY man cream, elbow trusting leg warmers, hero facilitating jet chords, word wanking whipperwills, Gif edging joyriders, farm fed anti-trolls, meat beating time bandits, hoodie flick and the jelly beans, her flic and the bonjour bonjours, toss me off and the good grades, elephant stones in my marmaljam.

There's two or three places where I never am, and I am not in any of those places...
at exactly the same time.

FIFTY-FOUR

Dobrý Deli, Wonderdust and The Sušenky of Doom.

"Dear Google, I am in Prague 7. Where is the nearest galaxy to me?"

The Andromeda Galaxy is two point four million light years away.
The light from the Andromeda Galaxy has taken two point four million years to reach Prague 7.
Do you want to order an Uber?

There are things which are good, and there are things which are bad.

The wicked dispatch lightly ciders to Daler Rowney complex nubs.
Too short to sharpen.
Hands off my Dobrý Deli.
I am Braille Kunitz.
I am Švejkian Cernunnos, master of the hunt.
Český kapr guided through the student bun.
Entrance free to suffragettes.
Kdo je to? Co je to?
Pomoz mi, Sisyfe!
My Gambrinus is lagging behind.
It does not know Brahman.
It does not read Flash Art.
It does not trust a woman who never eats biscuits.

My pub, my rules.

The Green Man, Pan and Edgar Allen Tonda,

suburban friendly at the foosball tableaux.
"God zooms!" Green Man preaches. "Zoom, means 'chill'. Like, 'God chills'."
His primary rule being,
"You start! I can't help you until you start! Just don't be mean or condescending to me. It makes me sad."

Kde je záchod? Kde je můj Nahý Banjo Band? Kde je Ratzinger and the card carrying, toe sucking celestials?

When the illuminaries congregate and share their pastel humour,
we as a nation cringe.
When the Krymská Kraken belches and the pivní sýr kicks in,
woe betide those down tide resting on the boar's black back.
Born tired, the slick, broke jester drinks to Karel Gott im Himmel.

He's got a fitness App 'cos his life sucks so bad.

"We know where you live. You're always there. For this we doff our caps. If we could say the same of ourselves, we wouldn't need the Apps."

Get off the tram, you silly man. Wake up and smell the Coffice.

Your first nature will soon be second nature.

Loose ties sink shirts, where glottals stop for tea,
in the Dobrý Delikatessen
where fashion goes to die.
And they would silence the rest of the alphabet for a Katz's pastrami on rye.

Create beautiful things.
Create in beauty.
Take thinking out of the process and make what you would like someone else to make for you, not what you would like to make for someone else.
They don't want that.

They didn't ask for that.
Take it back.
Smash it up.
Toss it out
and try again.

Be conscious of yourself. Ask yourself what's your agenda.
Make ar' great again!
Turn it into horses,
or 'How to learn this language in just ten days' courses.
Or seascapes or otters,
or relief from tremens deliriums,
or mermaid drag shows at the zoo in their glitter-bombed aqueeriums.

In me Žižkov deli. In me 'now' satori. In me I feel heliotropes of eternal love and devotion.
I'm dancing THROUGH the ceiling to Lionel Ritchie's chagrin, but he'll thank me when he realises the trap that he was in.

A nice cup of tea is the closest most people will ever come to calming the fuck down.
Philosophers are just very stupid people struggling to put Buddha nature into words. They are writing for idiots taught by idiots.
Look at the woods. The trees are connected.
Sigourney's weird in 'Alien Resurrected'.

"When I was a lad, some of me mates used their dinner money to buy whole packets of biscuits from the local shop. And they'd have that for lunch. Like thirty biscuits in one go.
That's NOT good."

FIFTY-FIVE

There's a Žižkov you know, and there's a Žižkov I know.
And then there is Žižkov.
No Hitler for you on this false Falcon's Crest telling time to the homeowners and sheet-white street settlers.
I know you have a gun.
I know you carry it to and from school in your satchel because you are afraid of being attacked because you live in Žižkov.
Ooooohhhhh, Žižkov!
You don't need a gun. You are invisible.
I don't remember your face two minutes after you leave the room,
you racist twonk.
People walk through you.
You have no substance.
You do not matter.
You wave your pistol around in front of us to impress the ladies.
Put down your gun.
Put yourself down.
You should use soap.
There's a Žižkov I know that reads like a cryptic clue,
and the answer does not include you.

Go straight on to Gottland,
under the balls of the one earth-eyed equestrian's charge,
not once turned round to see from whence it came.
Jiránek, the wrestler immortalised by not-that-Kafka
only five years before James Dean met his maker driving that unfortunate Little Bastard,
procured and heavy and light and crumply.
Object History, Subject utopia.
You should see what they've done to the park and the view,
and the Mercedes Benzes the Nazi children once drew.

And the communist heart I stole from the museum shop in the
vein hope that I would be noticed by the coppers and finally
earn the right to be labelled. Objectified.

"Give me an 'A'! Gimme an 'L'!
Wassat spell? Wassat spell?"

"*They used to tell me I was building a dream*
And so I followed the mob
They used to tell me I was building a dream
With peace and glory ahead
Now it's Al all the time...AL."

Your pal.

Part time communist-heart thief.
Part time singer on the scrounge,
with my Kickstarter, my inheritance, my dismissal of Ezra
Pound,
and a desire to learn how to play pinochle like Harpo Marx and
Alexander Woollcott at the Algonquin club
whilst balancing well, dressed, ex-patriot Russian poetry scenes
on beer mats knocked off from U Tunelu.

Luboš Plný pile drives my own overdeveloped Basquiat
imagery
into the Lennon wall.
I take a holiday snap that accidentally captures Vodník blowing
the Grey Man
outside the Museum of Military tools.
Coincidence?

U Vystřeleného Oka to U Slovanské lípy, Koněvova
to the old Žižkov tunnel,
we ate and played and kissed and stayed
and rounded up all of our distractions on the table in front of
us,
and flicked them like flat penguin discs
to catch spinning in mid-air,
till we had brushed away the cobwebs and could see each other

clearly.
Uncle Eugen and Aunty Marina telling beautiful anecdotes of
the days when they were werewolves
when werewolves were considered de rigueur,
and they shared a commune with other werewolves that made
art by day and grew art by night.
And still we flicked and caught the discs
and still the food kept coming,
and still the belief that we could live forever despite the sound
of sirens and the incessant beat of the little drummer boy
drumming.

Forty-two shopping days till normal Xmas.

And we did nice things and made nice stuff and liked each
other and wore good clothes.
And drank a lot and discovered lost things in impossible places
and bought more wine
and stocked up on beer from the nice man and nice lady
and the kid in the shop
and wondered if we weren't drinking too much,
and it's funny because I drink so much more than that now.

Friends all in the palm of one district.
Holešovice. Runner up model for paradise.

Oranges and lemons cure cancer.
It is a better place we are now than we have ever been.

It was the best of years, it was the worst of years AND it was the worst of years.

It was the year of the made-up plants, and it was the year of the Ayatollah Khomeini's sex change operation.

She has exquisite taste.
Your first questions should be on immigration
and the American detention camps and Syria or Afghanistan
or Libya or Iran and Israel and the U.S.A.
or the indulgences which lead to self-reprimanding behaviour

at not having spent sufficient time considering more pressing
matters than how to make the perfect hot dog
or where the next hot dog is coming from.

Put string around the rotten lot of us.
Keep us from falling down. Letting ourselves down.

Forty-two beer mats. A record. Big hands.
I can catch forty-two.
Get me a lawyer.
Let's make this official.

Scant soap operatics internment.
Wave crests breaking untimely.
Catch it in a poem a painting or an essay and riddle me this –

'You want to change the world? Why you make it so
complicated?'

FIFTY-SIX

Shooter's Island.
Miss Translation and Mister Opportunity collide in an
undocumented meet-mute on.

"Excuse me,"
says Mister Opportunity,
"I'm going for a piss."
"Did you just say 'piss'!!!"
laughs Miss Translation.
"Yes," laughs Mister Opportunity, simultaneously
understanding the truth of Wittgenstein's proclamation
that a serious and good philosophical work could be written
consisting entirely of jokes.

It can never be the job of the philosopher to 'reduce' anything
to anything,
or to 'explain' anything,
because philosophy is 'purely descriptive.

"I hate to use quotes," Mister Opportunity says, "only listen to
this..."
But Miss Translation has already left the building
to murder everybody who ever planned to say anything at all,
just in case
someone sometime
in the future
might choose to quote her.

How can something so easy be made to sound so difficult?
The key is in the question.

May all ordinary men be struck dumb.

Beauty can be so ugly.
Love is hate at the turn of a phrase.
The anatomy of language,
a Venom we may never control.

After she had murdered all the mouth talkers,
she took a bath and called her hairdresser to complain about
the bad man
and the terrible date,
and the state of the plumbing.

She's waiting at the wedding cake hotel,
fried icing sugar melting over the cemetery walls to read
excerpts of Kafka's private letters over his family grave.
I'm two hours late,
or she's two hours early,
or a little bit of both
and the scales tip in favour of love
as Mister Opportunity compulses a referendum.

'CouldSheBeTheOne?' part three.

FIFTY-SEVEN

Blinky Bellas. is visiting Dave and I.
B.B. is polished '95.
I am skating, and David is recruiting bricks.
In front of a downtown church
we are opening and closing BIG doors
and painting.
Though we are not moving.
And our hands are filled with beer bottles.

David is sketching alluring nurses on a delicious pale blue
background;
B.B. is painting abstracts with the acumen of a focused tempest.
David tells B.B. I have a small penis
and what else is he likely to say.
B.B. paints.
She asks about men and the things men do.
We ask them about women and what they do.
B.B. paints with a knife-shaped heart.
Pastel made strong Chimay.
Pilsner wants to polka.

Prague let them in.
Real in.
They stayed until they didn't,
and marked my dreams with a heart-shaped sword.

Prague painted real B.B.
I rolled up my sleeves and grew what little I knew.
A kind of freedom.

My principal to be questioning everything,
makes it hard for any of the other principals to stick.

There is no common ground today
for direct and simple understanding.
The answer lies in self-reflection.
Heidegger buys hisself a personality
and Effingham Huffnagle goes to the fairground.
Self-reflection is made more difficult because we have no clear,
common, and simple relation to reality
or to ourselves.
I mean to say, It's never been about race or religion,
it has always only been a question of varying levels of stupidity.

One last look out at the Ocean with the cry of seagulls in our ears,
and together we march into battle,
all of us against the one common enemy.
Time.

"I think I've got words inside me," they wake up and say, "Today I shall write at the Unplaceable Pew of the holiest church."
Placard reading,

JESUS
FANCIES
YOU!

They clamour alone,
wholly unimpeachable and rasp out their botanic winter wit
and wits.
And I love them.
"Summer is coming," they say,
and everyman knows it
but it's still nice to hear it
or read it
and I keep warm
with them.

They nurture nature with their creature features
and double bills
and direct their own movies because it's them what wrote 'em,
and they act in their own films

because it's all about they,
and everyman reaches over into my bag of popcorn
and I slap its wrist because it's my bag of popcorn.
It sinks back into its reclining cinema seat and takes off its shoes,
so its lying there next to me
as if at home,
and I'm looking at its filthy socks thinking that this expensive cinema experience is being ruined by everyman's feet.
And my sister is laughing hardest at the picture
and my sister is crying hardest at the picture
and we keep warm that way until summer arrives
and the pews have been reupholstered to look like forests
and Gillian tells me in the car 'Perhaps you are depressed,'
and it makes me cry,
in a good way,
and I change everything.

B.B. first out of the gate to show what it looks like when you art.
Edward Kirkby my literary electric rabbit,
Beeb my progressive possibility-sigil.
In-woke in-them I firstly saw,
the brilliant insta-soul mate Djinn.
The chaos magic symbols drawn from unconscious operating psyches.

Modern day warrior of godless refugees,
meming the grimoires
and hexing the foes,
giving birth to a general and painting his toes.

"Hamburger, but hold the burger."

Friendly fries and hold the cooks.
Unfolding the cosmos by cutting it short.
"Of course there is no meat in the salad,
of course not,
only chicken."

But the look in their eyes at the tangled truths and Illuminatory

cadences of the welcoming clubs
and the hand drawn pubs
and the friends who were yet to be glyphs
to be summoned in ceremonial futures.

Watch the way they...
see how they...
copy when they...
stop if they...

B.B. called London very 'forgiving',
and pretended not to know me on the Underground,
and I laughed when the passengers began to stare at me
as I tried to catch B.B.'s attention from across the carriage.
"Is this our stop?"
The Threshold missed by a hair's breadth.
A moment's alacrity.
A Robert's Shea. A Robert's Wilson. A Robert's Zimmerman.
A family plot in the land of nod
where the monkeys jibber jabber
and the policeman all smoke weed.

From St Martins to the tombs.
To the toppermost of the poppermost.
And Hacienda's in your treasure chest
and pirates up your sleeves
and a wardrobe you died for,
and a big hand to Marianne Faithful.

Every puzzle, every problem, every joy, and every surprise.
You never pretend anything.
Bold enough to improvise our rebellion in the hope that some cute,
unnoticed little mole might water us and nourish us
and see us blossom in its garden of earthly delights.
You are all the people I would want to be if I were not me.

Oh, but they got a shine like a magnificent graffiti tag,
with depth and work and honesty.
A newly excavated seal.

And a smile which makes you trust that every living creature
has it in them to be kind.
They listens with care.
Rare.

I dream you. Neat lines. Civilisation. World beginnings.
Affluence and Eve.
And you are safe. Born slippy. I was a ghost only you could see.
I now amplify your clemency.
On my good days.

Pull out all your stops.
Visit all your invented languages.
Aim your proofs towards the heavens
and micturate o'er the populist masses.

FIFTY-EIGHT

SCRUM

We had mainlined all the credentials on off-er, since sounds were turned to pictures – nice –
and a case was made for thinking
V
I
S
U
A
L
L
Y
...

'Describing' words all meaningless unless you count the brain that treats them to the time it takes to carve a love heart into the leg of a sailor.
Leggy / Appley / Bluey / Cakey / Clivey / Wiley / Firey / Watery / Airy / Earthy

......

"Thiz We Know."

...

We want to help. Help ourselves help others.
We look to those who helped us.
Artists and Mothers. I am not a practical man.
I find comfort in books

and bed.
To write books that bring comfort.
We might find happiness before we leave.
To paint a painting that will
bring calm,
quicken your heart,
kill your pain.
To create a work of art that will lift you up,
help you choose,
loosen your tongue
and let you see that there is so much more to life than art and books and bed,
and miles to go before all the artists are dead. Deal with it.

Sincerely,

Plum
XXX

...

I dreamt everybody died. And that was the end. It put a real dampener on my hard-earned philosophies.

...

Keep the kettle simmering, with ecstasy and fire,
and watch that kettle carefully so it doesn't boil over.
And while the kettle's simmering, be sure and get your oats,
and don't leave your ticket lying around for someone else to catch your gig.

...

Just so's we don't have to work our asses to the bone
we will rock you to sleep
with the chamomile-daily-waylays
off the beaten tracks of your pockmarked arms.
Drug Bentleys.
Dream Royces.

Sad guitars
and melancholy homegrowns is our remit.
'Avoid handstands' our motto.
Lazy as asphalt in a heatwave,
just cogent enough to talk to the languid winds mourning the death of activity.
Walks in 'the nature' approved by Friedrich.
A stroll along the unpeopled sands signed off by Ludwig.

If you hate Mondays so goddamn much why don't you P.M. the 2.7 billion users who 'liked' your post and plan a revolution for Wednesday afternoon. I'm doing nothing.
I can help out with the sandwiches.
There's a Spanish style bodega in the centre. We can get our wine from there.
For every peaceful naysayer,
a magnetic fork each and a packet of garlic Pringles.
For the undecided,
gift them a stuffed badger with the word 'unprejudiced' tattooed on their cleanly shaved sides.
You shall call the gathering 'Minds and Mouths Wide Open',
and there will be a massive tureen of Goulash soup for everyone to help themselves, and one tureen for vegetarians, like a goulash soup but with no meat. It won't be as good but...

Between the 2.7 billion of us I am sure we can come up with something more inspiring than 'Mondays'.

We'll know it when we see it.

...

"What you don't know can't hurt you." Communism.
"What they can't see can't hurt them." Botulism.
What you can't say can't be said.
Better post something on Fuckbook instead.
He threw the football way over all of our heads.
None of us got it.

...

In the crinoline corridors of his university structure,
broad shouldered and cast,
he sits in his soup of the day and gives his wares away
like a grand Teutonic poobah.
Coddling his library and auguring in the eschaton.
Inviting in a whole zinc of finches.

What sounded better when you were younger sounds better
when you're older sounds better now you're older what you
loved when you were younger.
I promise to do my best
to do my duty to nobody in particular or peculiar or groomed
by no adenoidal tattie drottle.
And if I should die before A.I. wake,
please wire me up and plug me in and keep me up to date on
the progress of our dutiful dynamic discord.
And frame me and put me up on a meth lab wall
witching the perimeter of aristocrats' mansion fences
and in the back alleyways of the I-Don't-Care-At-Alls.

Ahh, but a nice frame from a good framers.
Don't penny pinch.
Get up off your beautiful behind. Keep me in mind.
A frame which will embarrass all the false prophets
and tickle the underworld whilst simultaneously flipping the
proverbial proverb at all the wretched souls who believe goals
are the goals!

...

The scutters brought us together. Animal bits and bytes
conjured and soldered in retro spectacular by the war-shy
victims of this existential harvest.
In Farsi the Northern Lights look exactly the same.

...

But ugh ugh ugh that Shakespeherian rap!
The joy Beckett spoke of when he lead Cioran towards the
alternative light.

The light which is fun to imagine/remember when there is no light to be seen.
Or to be compared with when present.
Sound is motion.
Light is impossible.
Sight is metempsychosis.
One being's head with another being's body.
But still the same being.

...

We aliens flirting with semantics like bird dogs at a bacchanal.
Some girls are blither than others,
and then there's the Biblical, the Odyssean, the Koranic......
...the Satanic belch of an air bubble released from the belly of the Titanic,
rising, rising, rising...
pop.

...

We all get a go at the word-doxy.
No way to impregnate or get impregnated.
A two-way no-way street.
We are all safe.
And still we scribe the trull in order to find a way to meme those grimoires.

...

No point without immortality and no meaning without pointlessness...

[District Boundaries – No Access Beyond This Point]

...

Lambs to the sorter. They ain't never planned to kill us too quickly. Teach us about it first. Teach us what not to expect. And that's all. You taught me how to hate you. Oh God I hate

you. Oh Christ I hate you. Oh Allah I hate you. Oh Aslan I hate you. Oh Justice I hate you.
You false sponsors of a new dawn.

...

I am the shade of my shadow full flat on the path, basking behind the Babylonian obelisk of infinite variations.

...

The 59th Street Bridge Song to be played at my funeral.

FIFTY-NINE

The Descendants of Seth,
all lookalikes and porn stars,
collaborating Mennonite-lites foreshadowing the aeon of our
doubt and fact checking brethren
who we will keep in our pockets
and lendeth our digital granaries.
We are not born to hide.

Buddhist Monks and sundry ascetics unraining unsnowing
ungrowing.
No, we are not supposed to hide. But BILD BILD BILD.
And in doubt trust.

Make up your own mind how well the plenary eat,
and plow the fields and store your produce before the endless,
assiduous trollery brews, and names all the plants and seasons
and animals for you.
Each to their own ark,
their primula-screen denouement,
the beginning and the ending in one square light,
and out there...
out there they is all in error, and in chaos they will remain,
while my family and my ark alone shall save the innocent
with awesome tweets and funny gifs
and if you pledge a dollar or more
I'll share your crappy websites.

...

Mercury muffled,
his eyes Dylaning round and around from the swans to the
ducks to the cops and geese

and red squirrels think they run the place
now the city is empty.
The natural order of things unnormalised,
while the roach-ridden bars await their roach smoking poets.
We capitalise on nothing as our doomsday predictions provide
for themselves; double down on melancholia and have nothing
left to say.
I would learn to be a doctor,
but everybody's dead,
I would learn to be a fireman,
but the newly inspired, territorial quackers took the oxygen.
I would learn to speak another language
but one is not enough to unravel the multitude of ways we are
destined to misunderstand each other.
And everybody who is anybody becomes nobody forever.

The lily and the rose, the word and the friend,
your delirium and rain wine,
teetotal flirt rebellion and antidisestablishmentarian race
against pot-bellied left-wingers mincing about.

...

Don't ask her where she's from, she won't tell you. Don't ask her
what she does, she can't say.
An old teenager in a beanie
from a bed in the warehouse goes to the head,
makes you dribble like an infant as you crawl to the shops
and ask for clemency and Zuzu's petals.
There will be no Christmas this year
and the weeks and months and days blur into one,
like you always wanted,
and you don't want it anymore.
Po' boy. No money, no time, no religion –
this is what it feels like to be ornery.

Just be careful what you ask forfurtherfatherfor.

You are going to get everything you ever dreamed of.
How this works?

You ask – you get.
They ain't leaving no sad cowgirls and beat guitar strummers,
fists clenched behind their backs to foot-pen their letters of complaint come judgement day
on the fourth of November
when the chasm yawns and we are hit with the halitosis of our collective dream-sewers' lava mulch.
Shit rising to the top
and one hundred and fifty-six people televised jump.

ENDITALLS.

You are not safe in your future visions.
You have it in you to make yourself safe.
You know you can make yourself safe.
It's that easy. But you don't do you?
You are a twenty-four-second-minute enabler.
You are a Melania colluder.
Your gnashers are smoothed on the bones you be grinding.
Your night terrorists pulped and kerranged into immortal policies
removing all possible religious questioning on the grounds that the Lord, merciful protector of all worlds
has lady balls.

Stop hiding behind this mirage of oppression
which you, yourself, an able-bodied, dull-witted apologist
are sketching and photographing and printing in order to create something from nothing.
Something from nothing.
A painting of a mirage solidifies the mirage in the mind of the viewer
and bullies them into giving the image a name which it does not require, deserve or want,
or know how to want because it is NOTHING!

just

like

your

god.

Play old playschool trumpets and strike up the band,
Glen or Glenda Miller style,
and have Hamell on Trial tail-tamed sing to me of bygone days
so we can reflect in poesy over sweet sherry and a first Panatela.
All those cosies and snugs.
How beautiful the wars was when men were women, and
women were women, and life wasn't worth a tuppence fennig.

"If nobody showed up then there would be no war – The flag is
a mirage painted in horse blood – Last night – When we were
young."

"It's not that simple," they will tell you. "It's just not that simple."
And you believe their lie,
and you just know they will die for their right to believe in
belief.

A person gets bored.

You are not factoring in the boredom that not-fighting-strangers brings.
There are only so many role-playing games a guy can bear
before he's curling his eyebrows and colouring his hair,
naming the fruit in his fruit bowl after Spice Girls and former
Derby Stakes Run winners,
and his wedding cutlery after Mutant Ninja Turtles.

Oh lord, merciful protector of all worlds,
make us nicer and better at words and gooder at proving you
mean less than nothing without us having to waste our precious
breath in the process.
Phonemes,
graphemes,
logographs
and salt tossed over our giant shoulders into the wind

whenever one of your million names barges its way into 'grown up talk'.

No Dada joke absurder than Takfir.
To excommunicate a Muslim – to create an infidel.
To create an infidel – to insult the supremely sensitive creator.
Better to kill the non-believer dead,
or torture them 'smart'.
Or torture them until thinking for them-self
They become morally reprehensible.
This philosophy clearly only remotely defensible,
If ones only alternative to 'believing'
is to be beaten
insensible.

And Azadeh spring forths solubabble happenworths.
A polarising witch watch on a slim pretended bus.
A chance to plot the manygaps.
A hope to blot the blottoed.
A universal antidote to danceless cronyism.

Az' pitches and punts and opts for the cake one.
Not the plain one or straight one
or the 'get one for free' one.
Exquisite.
She elbows and leaps and fights at the drawbridge
of dutiful jobsworths soiling their thawbs.

Empties her paper bag of potraviny felt tips and busies herself
colouring in the gates outside Radio Free Europe.
Now she's high fiving the guards.
Now she's making them lunch
with an alpine smile the size of entire families reunited.
The streets light up. Here we are safe. In the soft, delicate hands
of the truth sayers and the ambassadors of memory.

'Woman. Life. Liberty.'

SIXTY

Generation X.
Generationless.
A Gerontion-tinged, birth of binging.
Binging words and cigarettes and alcohol
and acid and ecstasy and speed
and weed and coke out of reach for these grunge pyjama
delirials.
T-shirt revolving syntax pimps.

Meanwhile she all cat wet scales roofs big glass reading apple.

Makes she video art force space aim trumps famille article noise tears.

Shed beer mug mat joke book Henry James Diary of a Man of Fifty.

Gut German rung-a-dink Microscopical gluten-pliny the elder.

Firesign mensch urban Goethe public display of affectation.

I'll go in the rain unlike you I have nothing to do a megaphone could come in handy one day.

Ambition comes with a gun in its hand borrowed from Han Solo good looking white noise.

Outside the castle stayed the hesterglock Czech culture moist and praying castle.

30th Oct – 1st November macro binary corpuscle nomads

relish-relic white bedroom seance sauce (pronounced sa-oos).
What is smores? What is smores? what IS SMORES?

M'aidez. Mayday. M'aidez.

Gabba gabba

hey.

...

The kitchen tote bag full of paperbacks returned to the scene
of the crime.
Marketa, Marketa, don't judge me too harsh.
I was young.
Tummy-stupid.
I screamed out front your window. Your living room top the
granary.
I screamed expletive high and mooty.
Stoopid show-off fol-de-riddle de-riddle de streets.
My ungrateful tribe.
Selfish Spanish orange thought.
If you were here now that night, I would apologogogise just
enough
for the city we were in
which is not now.

W
A
S
P
We are so proud.
Women and slick pensioners.
WOLT a Sosostris prick!
Why are seniors proved?
Water and sand pain.

I like to listen to Freewheelin' Bob Dylan when I lose all sense of
sense.
And everything I hurl at myself I hurl in hope of dissipating

a Jesusing lifetime of complimenting the unworthy and unfriendly.
And dissing the undeserving.
One wrong syllable.
Never trust a hippy.

SIXTY-ONE

Armand wry-smiles.
An emoji cajoling the crowd.
Uncle punch bag spermtacular!
Old Tom Moore in all the stories. I don't care. In all the stories.
In the days of.
Ragshack Bill spills his guts online and Louis schlurps them up,
sober good.
Predicted the comeuppances of when the slow reply.
Yes that's fine. It's a wrap.
We'll take that one,
thanks.
Good egg. Schlurpey egg. Chickenegg.
Wood-knot-pecker's never gonna finish this art project till you
murder yourself in the first degree and accept that this is not
what you want to do
but you have no choice
because this is the only thing you ever really wanted to do.

"Take a stand against yourself and tell yourself to shut the fuck
up, you whinging little cunt.
Go to bed and leave the safety off your lately born rifle."

Sologomy be damned!

And one evening for pleasure
I walked with her down some river they wrote a song about
all whimsical and famous,
dead long and double good.
And parting from my promise, worried over that river for the
sake of a girl.
Soz, Dave.
It was meant for you.

If this promise was a decoration I could send to you now
it would be on a big, big, red rock typewriter
like I seen them yoopsters recreate
in glued suede shoos,
On T.V.
in Pyjamastan.

...

"Don't make me write another line. Don't make me write another
line, don't make me write another line. Don't make me write
another line. Don't
make
me."

...

And don't fall for the person who makes you feel like you just
wrote the last line.
Hanging over you,
every syllable you mutter,
you fucking imbecile.
Love is the syllable which will kill you.
The slow walk in the fresh air to the suicide bridge
because this IS the bridge where your partner makes you feel
like a phoney for the very last time.

The Nusle Bridge which we can see from the kitchen,
I swear harbours rocky harbours.
Maybe that's why the tenants all leave in dark therapeutic
relinquishing deaths. Maybe that's why nobody can sleep here
without nightlights
or candles or angels or crystals
or miniature fairy castles,
or better still,
Katarína Bakošová whose voice tiptoes in to whisper you all a
"Sladké sny,"
on a Simona Macková gossamer snowboard frottage.
Lilo lilting in concrete disguise
of solid tear drops buttered.

Pulcritudes' light motif with teeth.
Sightseeing Hades with rose tinted binoculars, compiling
soothing regiments of a hemp healers' wish list,
whilst singing the anthem you would adopt if you alone were a nation.
Female Caliban in a Shawn the Sheep costume

Glitch.

A Fauvist Meep.

You were always on the way. It is always close.
But, closer now, closer...closer...

You're in advertising?
So go ahead, kill your sons!
The rising moon is only the end.
The bowl of fresh oranges and smoke fairies.
On your yellow IKEA table.

Name dropping is gauche.
The word gauche is gauche.
Czechs say gauch instead of couch.
That's different.
Let's celebrate our differences,
if that doesn't sound too gauche.

SIXTY-TWO

The shaggy dog and the baffled proletariat,
the cuddly toy and the humblest witch in Sardonia,
beautiful, them-versions.
The expressionist victuals currying favour in spice-filled
cellars groaning with masturbating Mickeys and fornicating
Republicans rubbered.
Foreign stuff with music in red.
Masking tape and light sabres and excrement and butt-faces
after the title, rarely before.
Rarely done, not underdone,
Sandinista, corpulent garrisons, war time bunkum,
civil warring agent provocateurs straying from the festival of
the unacceptable
with a handshake and a tapered grin,
trying to get back in by the light of the silvery moon
and moog synthesiser wank stains in your elephant ear
welcome mats
bloodied and chaos dolls.
Just one step further through the bony church of your hateful
sensibilities
and they spike you in the heart and brain with a metatonic
mutational shock.
Apple sauce reasoning in Grandma's oiled pants.
Tits tasselled undulate
and careening in the name of all unsaid, unholy,
unwed
out of dire unviable respect for unwarranted longevity.
...

OP II

Cactussy. Beneath the stern serenity of Masaryk's bespectacled

portrait
we breakfast catapulted from smudge-face to laughter lines,
snow white as Jan's horsey hair,
yellowing as her perfect eggs yellowed,
frightening as her perfect day smudged frightens.
Coffee-nervous,
word-nervous
and squinting hard to massage my temples.
Tentacles gangly and electrified and clustered in a folio of
misread signs and disease-ridden hot tub nests.
Neck nine months stiff.
Lower back moping in earnest.

...

I am a compromise.
Je suis un compromise.
Já jsem compromise.
Ich bin eine compromise.
Mil jan sec colollo, loco.
As soon as pen touches paper the poet and the poem is
compromised.
As soon as a poet thinks their first thought and 'words' it,
the poet, the poem and the thought are compromised.

At its worst poetry is the compromise of truth and the
compromise of beauty.
At its best poetry makes no claims.

By magnets vicariously magnetised.

...

Struggling for every breath
when breathing is the easiest thing for us to do.
godmade-easy.
Focus on your breathing and don't think about your breathing.
Be honest with yourself but don't make a big deal out of it.
Exercise by doing things which exercise the body without it
being exercise.

A plant asks for water without asking.
The body does what it does.
Talk to poets and artists about anything but poetry and art.

Don't sit in my hall looking through the frosted glass into my bedroom.
Knock knock or fuck off.
Be honest with yourself but don't say anything.
The universal alphabet in silent stages.
Brought to life by the inimitable Grace Kelly and James Stewart.
From a distance.
Then closer. Then closer. Glen close.
Bunny mad. Thrice bitten – very shy.
A film by Shakespeare's great great great grandtrouble.
Should have been a landslide.
They like him BECAUSE he's an evil dictator. Bunny raper. Too close.
Make amends.
Be here how.
Who we're.

I remember Trafika and colourful, peopled magazine troughs.
I remember Yazzyk and lady chemists in white socks and white sandals.
I remember *The Prague Review* and lady waiters in stained white socks and white sandals.
I remember (UNPRONOUNCABLE SYMBOL) and what star sign are you?
I remember *Prognosis* and attractive unattractive cafe cliques,
I remember Litteraria Pragensia and dog-eared kids who kept 'journals'.
I remember *The Prague Post* the dirty river still dirty river.
I remember *Provokator* and baby steps towards Kevin's Bacon.
I remember names but not faces
and faces but not names
and
I remember those were pearls and eyes and music slowing down and movies slowing down in a state of pink Russians and microdots

and approaching casting director Beth Gibbons, or was it Nancy Bishop,
with our idea to put on a play.
'The Drinking Party'.

We would begin by wearing smart suits like fifties gangsters.
We would become gangsters.
We would sell wholesome British fare and call it Dave and Mike's Sensible Food.
We would import Branston Pickle, Scotch Eggs and Salt and Vinegar Crisps.
We would put our 'sensible' food inside Rohlíky instead of sausages and call them 'Rollicking Good Rohlíky'.
We would invite famous people to get drunk with us, sleep over, and in the morning prepare for us their own special hangover cures.
We would film all of this and call the TV show 'Mike and Dave's Famous Hangover Cures.'
We would take acid every day.
We would never let a girl come between us.

SIXTY-THREE

'The alchemist should be discreet,
revealing to no one the result of their operations.
They should choose their days and hours for labour with discretion.
They should have patience, diligence and perseverance.
They should avoid having anything to do with princes and noblemen
and they should be sufficiently rich to bear the expenses of their art.'

Alex Went is a gentleman.
In the alchemical dungeon of Napa I read from The Refusal of Silence.
I am an alchemist now.
Alex is English with a capital city. Alex is nice.
Nancy Bishop is there. She is also nice.
I remind her of a twenty-five-year-old pitch. She doesn't remember. Might have been Beth Gibbons.

An alchemist must be discreet.
They should avoid anything to do with princesses and nobility.

To think of the Rumblefishes already out there plying their trade,
unpaid hourly by the day
and sleepless night in an adjutants bigup
at the helm of a predated anomaly-wish.
A wide wish warm in an overnight success-onesie.

We weren't married to the idea anyways.

The dragons swoop in and knit the copulating future-past

avant guardians,
lit right by beaconing volary,
Dan Kenney. Globe food alchemist.
Thinking and walking and talking.
Finds me writing at the bar of the Lucerna Cafe,
post penurial dawbings in their (UNPRONOUNCABLE SYMBOL).
A wickeder mojo he'd purport to relay,
and grilled to a man-size think-tank.
He very-humaned,
and catapulted pretentiousness out the portholes of our colloquially same submarine without getting any of us salt hills wet.
Dan Alchemist. Alex Nobleman. Bishop a bishop.
Watch out the en passant.
Watch out the triple fork.
Watch out the gambit declined.
It might pepper your mercurial cigarettes.

Today I am the Knight of Pentacles.
I write without revision.
Leave the details to 'Future' Mike.

I sleep most of the afternoon with the balcony door ajar.
There's a bug on my wall. Next to the bed.
Instead of writing, I am deciding whether or not to leave the bug,
or use a glass and scoop it off the wall to toss it outside.
I write this down so future Mike won't feel like he wasted the day.
This is what wasting the day looks like.

At the end of the tunnel my left eye stares into my right eye and infinity blows itself.
From the stage eyes and audience satchels I pace back and forth pinning words with a shaky hand.
But there at the back of the room.
There in the dark recesses of the decade...

There's Sasha Rose and Yeva Kupchenko

heralding the mascots weaved from train track dust
and the dry sneeze of a boll weevil.
With the grace of atom-free bombs they hem the caverns'
poetic redresses
with alluring simplicity;
complexing the empty space in a dialect saved for the initiated.

Eli Anders casting her cumulus collages on the lit womb walls
of our literary leviathan.
Busying the overlooked moments which never pass her by
and so she shares her notices,
arms akimbo and Venus-hair pointing in the direction of 'You
should fucking care!'
as bicycle after bicycle joins in the fun
of the multi-action art farm
market thinky brazen sexy cattle run.

SIXTY-FOUR

I knife John Waynes in my pyjamas.
Republican spin doctor gunning with the Love Priests
burning in the twelve suns.
Ellington the topper Duke.
The violin is hard to play,
and I listen to my flatmate run up and down the stairs
ploughing through the hardatit.
Cobalt blue hair flowing in solar wind and the queer sounds of Valinor.
Her evening morning and afternoon loolooby.
She does not believe in Corona
but if the 45th president gets a second term, I may join her
waxing and waning mooning in the elven realms of esoteric bubbles
cartomancing the cellars of sparkle pony nectars.

I will become a fantasy book.
Thirty-nine crown Tesco Merlot. Stay drunk.
Imaginary-shaft those Donkey Fascists with my fantasy wand fuckstick
from my socially distant fantasy back pages
and waft them screaming into oblivion;
apologise to oblivion;
usher them back and shaft them again
because I know I cannot do this alone.

Know your enemy.
In the sick biblical sense.
Fuck a racist.
Fuck a racist today.
I could have fucked a racist.
Spite fuck.

Like the violin.
And my gauntlet of troof
and my cloak of indivisibility
and my bucket of shells collected from the nice beaches I walk
along at sunset in the undying lands
to give to you to put on the mantelpiece for us to look at when
we sit together in the evening reading something good
and drinking sweet hot chocolate with ginger,
special,
like only you make it.

...

There are no meetings. There are only meetings.
No one caves. Only you.
I'm no Henry James.
My beauty is in the implications.
I blame my educations.

...

Livin inna werld wur a differen song at da end of every episode
is considered INTELLLLIGGENT TV.
Sink about thaaaa...
......

The cunt loses. The cunt goes to play golf. I call Jo and
me Mum. Me Mum tells me the Russian cunt might have
Parkinson's and will leave in January too. I message Jo with
the news article about the Russian cunt. Jo sends two Gifs. A
surprised Jimmy Fallon,
and a surprised cat.

...

Malcolm XXX meets in iron gate park tunnel with Bichop
Babwith
in a Fication of Villumses.
One has bringed a red flower for romance.
The Bichop.

Malcolm puts the rose in his ear.
The way out of their temperbutt is out the squeezy middlerun.
A love of words and a hate of words is not enough to light their revolution.

Light is un oeuf.

Shake off all that filthy feline flotsam and geriatric jism, ya mangy dog,
there's a strawberry blonded mot with a portable terraformer in her Mucci purse-purse up ahead,
now get on your knees and beg for it, bub 'an stooooopppppp countin'.
An m-fest vodka vision,
semi-periphereled cute mutt waste spreader tactic.
Still, that head of hair. Still that.
I'm all in 'ND one day,
not-wet,
will sit to chew his text 'N unravel the code that is Garcia,
discuss Anger and Crowley and R.A.W.
and the miserliness or altruism of provocation.
...

So the mook base.
It can wait.
Down here may be okay.
For a while.
Mook Base Alpha.
Huzaaaahhhhh!

And a play is the cliche of a thousand plateaus.

SIXTY-FIVE

A local Lazy Fucker lying on the floor of the Horoměřice Titty Twister
playing dead to the out of towners
come to Beadle about our bawdy bar.
Míša,
my tumultuous, rat-loving army candy,
lips soft as brass,
pounces.
I have her back.
The scuffle ends as weakly as it had begun,
not with a bang but with many many swear words.

'Shit', 'Shit you!", "Shit on you, you motherfucker!", "Shitty fuck on you, you shitfuck!", "Bastard dick!"
and I am become an honorary member of 'Hat'.
Stood my ground,
and a round.

Accused of favouring all but Czechs in the Maastricht Treaty
despite a clear disparity in ages,
and reality,
and political affiliations.

Universalist.
I'm painting it large in David's barn
and drinking till I feel the harm.
But tracks lead me dragon tame to old ways and reprobates.

Mike C, a flasherback to a hoopier time.
A renegade lack of television, or world cares
or tinsel wishes in Columbine textless days
when trench coats Russianed their way into our uniform

and his face is a balm...remembers.
Vltava tip offs and the nonchalance of a beachcomber.
His doorman poker-face for Daniel's Craiglist unt Stormtrooper
jammy bugger kismet songs we used to sing before our hearts
were demanded.
His non same got lease for this place boss race question saint.

I mean how could she?
I mean why would she?

I mean I'm not sure if I remember this right
but there was a canon always in the undercarriage of Santa's
Spanish made sleigh and you never saw Christ masses so idyllic
as the Christ masses in this heathen enclave.
He recalls with no more smiles left.
No nostalgia.
He is sick of the memory game
and wants to say to those who went away,
"Why why did you leave me here with the types of fuckers
who never leave places after they left a place for good to be
somewhere like there's somewhere to be?"

Dave kills the fascist that is memory
in glibber doctrines than Mike has glommed.
Perhumps. Perhumps not.
I might not never know.
No one can be depleted in a city so thinning.
And creep I go
and fall into and turn
into the art shop next door but one two three on Pštrossova
and it is there my new life beganagain.

SIXTY-SIX

Waddle tent drum-tent to a rope in unitalic net irony pumps.
In busses' clefts and shindig argumentarian helms.
Wronguns and bad lefts.
Dark alleywinds.
AndsoIreturn.
Masturbating to Tracy Barlow uncoronated.
Brigadeens and unctuous friendly fraks, nooning the safehome.
Illustrating a bitty Karma bribe
for just a cigarette more and I'll quit one day.
An artless time illustrated by a love that should have.
Pounding on the church window, "You lied! You lied!"
A reasoned culture is a reasoned culture.

Of chloroformed deep dives at Sandy Cove and Donnybrook
and thirty foot
and mad bastards covered in goose fat
drowning their educations within earshot of Martello tower
page burnings.
I sit and watch families play
and think of Joyce's fantasy Brayolage, carnallic love-abortions
in curly sandworms;
a future face of all I ever wanted.
I went to the top of that tower all ticket-paid
to weaken the joy-jolt and wondered woonly
about salubrious James and bellicose Buck.
I sat in the fly away Saint Peter and fly away Saint Paul Basilica
today
and tried to channel God (The God)
with unequalled ineptitude.

I can't remember all the times I've told myself to hold on to a
moment

like it is a moment to keep sacred.

Like I'm a ninja like me Nanna who gifted me my first pack of
Taro Tora Taro Tora T.
And Mum, me first Dennis Wheatley.
I was a black magic prodigious, prodiginous calligraphy,
in the backstory shadow moment of a fourth-eyed Hillier.

"'Oh Rats!', the hero exclaimed, and I was out," says Peter.
So I'm out too, because "Rats!", I mean!

Francis Bacon's repositioned studio, my second home.
Andrei Tarkovsky's biggest fan, my gardener.

A future echo of me and some kids playing chess,
of all things,
on Elaine's balcony,
and a story about how David V. can famously play chess whilst
famously playing seventy-eight other games at the same time,
in his sleep, blindfolded, in twelve other languages.

"Tell us the one about David," my little angels will ask.
"Tell us the one about the Milky Way and how the cosmos
swore to be his cake-lennon."
"Not till you are both of age, poppets. No geniuses till then," I
shall say,
and we put the Christmas tunes on farrrrrrrrrrrrrrrrr too early.

Some think more than a hundred moves ahead.
I think one letter at a time.
That's why none of what you say makes sense to me,
or my red red robin soldiers who get off on my…

"Wait! Get off my cloud! Okay, but just move over. Shift up.
Don't worry. Stay there." "It's a cloud! It's only a cloud."
"Yeah, Happy Holidays to you too. And your King."
"Kin?"
"Yes, that's what I said."

My words have decided you.

I
am gone.
"What do you think of this pink" she says
holding up the pinkest pink you ever saw
in cuckold pinch-crime looks of Mandragora,
plagiarising hearts and purposefully ambivalence.
Pštross Výtvarné Potřeby Art Supplies supplying more than we
ever bargained for.

Jitka. An also colouring-in.
A red toothed, black-haired dolomite
pressing untimely, clawed coffee
till her wild-weed restaurant on Opatovická slows time down.
Boyfiend in tow,
tries to steal Dave's Frenz Experiment right from under our
Gnosis;
right from out my coat pocket.
I see him slipping it into his accessory friend's bag as I return to
the table.
I steal it back when he goes to the toilet.
Could have gone one of two ways.
Jitka's gang kicking my tongue down my hobnailed trouser-
throat.
Or else I'm embroiled in friendships favourable to the titty
twisted night hawk within.
Obsolutely we became friends.
Seen us be bad. Glean past new.
Task Jason tally spew,
and wotnot.

In The Globe framing readers too too devastatingly self-
educated.

"What do you recommend for a short break,
a long ride,
a bad head,
a good bed,
a Di dead,
a well read,
a pink square invited there and slowly inaugurated?"

Inauspicious stalker pals as strong as pals are strong.
Riddling addresses in tinted glasses.
Steining our duel exhibition in Slavia sellvia, shopping arcadia.
Shop drunk daily front wall space.
Tesco brand alimentarian visits.
Children draw copies of our copies of our story board
implementations of parentless townies.
A brother sister monument to friendship.
Eye-chewy and happy times.
I pen a whole novel for yoopsters with these two as the heroes
in a gothic underwater adventure of very little consequence.
Carpet burritos and our Bad Art project.
Deliberate Bad Art.
To make something with no aesthetic value whatsoever.
Much easier to make something bad if you set out to make
something good.
Camera Lucida.
Caught falling. Call waiting. Who will survive in this
underwater world?

I fraggled the meat-let got moundy.
She wexed the maiden set mutton.
He creeped the maddlerot and bled collated.
He wung and flail when I vexed.

Better that way.

SIXTY-SEVEN

There's a tingling sensation that something is being said.
Hoping and preying a sentence well lead
can tuck all the tunnelling sundries tightly up in bed at night.
Bugs biting, illumititing,
stop the fighting;
most conflict based on aural apparitions
and kennelled into our blood the moment we blink.
L.A. meets L.A.
A ruptured self-slif.
Groans about his owned homes' lubricated,
razor boobied garbage shoots.
Galadriel humps the Sasquatch of leftovers in the basement
but rapidly births new festooned literature, romantic,
fantastical, ectoplasmic, placentined quadrupeds splooged out,
standing up.

"Mummy! Mummy! I got grit in me gums." Undigested poetry
clogging the mammelmouth.
"Mummy! Mummy! Lemon-fix-scurvy!" The nomencreature
words like a beautiful incision in the skin (a wound by any other name),
vinegared and salted and promptly ingested,
suspecting thought perfected can still be bested.

Pseudo politic anarchocreeps
creeping into metaphysical meta-tombs and making like zombies
to destroy unwitty passers-by.
Cronyism now pregnated.
Solipsism geriatricked into thinking for others
then changing everything back again.
Intern issues with the level of access they are given to prep for

their new position as people of wealth.
The pan pipes warble in the downstairs room of his mind
palace, irritating him into a deep deep slope.

Jo puts on a show.

Peter and Wendy observe Jo's footstomp laterally
and reason the brainstorms back and cumulous.
Jo calls to her Woodstocked-Roksan-conscience at the piano
climbing the C-hall walls in black and in white
and sometimes red
and the singular intensity of a woman with a mission.
Her mission?
"To provide the worreld with an app which can toll yew how to
fax a prooblem if yew jast pint yourrr phone at the prooblem."
I, paraphazing homously.
Assem applauds the tenacity. Hanalisa cheers her britches.
Jessica breens at her pocus and Louis arrives three hours late
so can't qualify for the app, patented in a very small country you
won't have heard of yet.
Nor app.

Meanwhile, previously, excuse me, and so... excuse me...
the communion is held...excuse me, Žižkov...the communion is
held behind the Albert near Husinecká
in a rain Bob told us all
was gonna fall,
I knew it, he told you, he said, over and over again, no one ever
listens.

Jan photomaps all the transubstantiationaries to beat the band.
The police come cap in hand (for pregnant women's piss).
Jaromír brogues them with a sloppy kiss, typed.
Thor magics the room in recyclin' shorts and black glove
accusations,
"Sitting Ducks...Sitting Ducks...You are all Sitting Ducks..."
and we carouse and we shop and we stay till the final sacrilege.
Asgeir claims the Beatles are overrated and I blow a gasket.
Pretend like. Fun like. Anna picks up the pieces and recites
them back together again

at Santa's grebby grotto.
I am learn-ed and can deal with difference of opinion.
I am learn-ed and can deal with differences of opinion...

"Pint your phoone at 'em, and repeat ad nauseum..."

Warm sitting ducks.
I, Jan and Thor speak of family and war
and lift the children onto the cupboard above the kitchen
counter to keep them safe from harm,
and the cat goes there too, by choice, for perspective,
to be bigger, to be safe.

There are no thresholds and everything is in vinegar.
I jot down our plans with an inky chopstick dipped in quails'
eggshells filled with donkey ink transferred to melty rice paper
and start all over again.

SIXTY-EIGHT

Sun map tropes.
I remember places not names.
No Jungian-Demian trip for the likes of us.
We are too innocent now.
We began fucked up.

Reverse analysis. The last thing I will see.

The room I will be in. The street I will be in. The hospital I
will be in. The forest I will be is and has always been the vision
which has dictated my love.
What the teachers' threw.
What stuck on me and stuck on you.
My death mask magnet in my adolescent acquiesce.
I will let this in.
I will seek that out.
Of this I want more.
The truth a tipping truck.
A topsy turvy nostalgia for the future when I shall need to know
no more.
Impasse reached and all the things I tried to gather
in my own samsarasatchel saturated.

My audience, Goth-Girls and women who were once Goth-
Girls.
By the time time zingers,
there I will be pure. Dark.
If you are listening,
I am already dead.

Author's default state – The Seven of Pentacles / The Moon /
The Hermit

Grounded and whistfoul.
Puzzled and monstered.
Crony bulb stone rose snow sixtacles clinging to our dangling ballsacks
in dog food for humans
and a wild mut-attack.
Tom, Dick and Harry rolled into one integrity.
Star farmer thinks like James Mason spoke.
His mute bush wobbles at all humanity's potential
and a brisk but simple beat to plan by.
Logan and his witch finder huddled.
Glancing over their shoulders while I stood at the door.
Making their decision.
"No."

The eternal mystery with its back to the answer.
Fallward thinking necrophylliacs,
clubbing up in a second-hand bookstore.
The Deep-YMCA of our lobster crush.
Will we ever get over the comfort of sorrow?
Arms pushing right ways but the stomach unaided collapses hope.
Arms resting heavy on the staff
and the path
and we want to do good
but not just yet.

Running swift-stood,
giving out to the sun mooning above.
The light of the cosmos is the light of the wise fool
is the light of his tunic and moccasins melancholy
crying over his own achievements.

Now where's the sense in that?
To have finished your work.
There is no more work.
To worry over what to do next.
There is only no more work.

We work backwards to our inevitable unstudied demise.

Look at what we will have.
Don't look back.
Look around you. You are on your death bed again.
What do you see? What do we eat?
What do you remember? What do you want to do tomorrow?
Impossible question.
Skipping food to pay for energy bills.
Nobody won the election.
We are alone on the platform.
What do you want to look like when that angel passes by
on the other platform
and looks over at you
and reflects on your story as they heave their backpack off,
settle onto their empty bench
and pull out a home-made sandwich
and a flask of spring water from a side pocket?

Two one-way trains.

She talks about stress into her map.
You fret about stress into her map.
You get your own map.
It's a sun map trope.

When the names are written down you can remember the names.
The places speak for themselves.
And she looks down, and you look down
and the moon looks down brighter than the brightest day
raining tears in a clear sky.
Opposite chairs.
Same map.
Your only hope now is the creature from the deep.

To stir the soldier of your heart which pumps on and on and on.
I would take your yucca and hostel key
but for the blue blood left inside of me.
I can't hear your footsteps. There is no sound in Arcana XVIII.
A mute card for a mute date;
one that has and hasn't happened already yet.

The only chance the author has of getting his end
is by getting The End.
And getting dark.
And Mome-Rath-reddening from out the seas depths
where the mettlesome curious dig upwards for their gold.

SIXTY-NINE

This Bag Kills Fascists.
I have the patients of a saint.
There's a reason you can see yourself in great art.

...

To be posthumous or not to be posthumous? That is a question.

As mysterious as fifteen minutes.
Or a bird of prey which is not a bird of prey.
James Stewart being massaged at the window.
Personal effects affects.
And the dog sniffs at the cold autumn ground for the body he buried not six hours ago.

...

Overture – Underdone.

Go where you are welcome. Don't go where you're not welcome.
Callback to pink.
Drink, drink drink...now consider yourself one of us.

Rosewah Earlybird open-haired wave waked naturally songbirding,
a dote control in thermal tandem with patience and glacial certitude, sistermotherwifing the highest fidelities
and soft paws for thoughts for lending a hand
when the going gets tough
and we need lifting off the hot hot sand.
She is built to catch and share the spill,

definition of will wrote the text,
reknitted the welcome mat,
embroidered the text into the welcome mat and opened the
proverbial gates-before-the-law.

Prague Film and Theatre Centre brewing to the metaclaps
of promptly sharp,
cashless bonding
knowingly captured up up up the stagehand's claypole lickety-
split,
and a ring around the.
Cheap theatre funerals,
cheap theatre weddings,
and cheap fantasies rolled out, dreamed up, and put on display
for the price of a ne'er you mind.
We don't pay and we don't pay in kind.
There is a love which binds you and runs deeper than petrol,
that will carry you foodlessly workhouse and Cratchett.

Undoctrinated first players cadge this artist and layabout
and cast him trimestered unbecoming to a mood-age.
Happy as Larry.

"Oh wheeeeeeere is loooooooove? Oh wheeeeeere is
sheeeeeeee? Will I ever know the sweet hello which is only
meant for meeeee?"

And the deadworkhorse inside amazed.
The punctilious demonstrative of the happiest dramaturge
profile fruit seasoning
and eye-catching Peanut.
Lucy Van Pelt and the gorgeous gamut of actors who before
anything, love of theatre put.
Namely, numeralogically and nominally,
she's a golden collapse of moving power with the childlike glee
of an unlaced shoe. You dance and risk everything for a show
at the level of a violet spirit singing at the top of your lungs.
Every whisper a cajoling mass of friendly impertinence adopted
by those closest to you,
that they may embrace your resilient amplitude.

Abby supplying reassuring pragmatism ropes come
angel-hearted magician bags, technically inviting humble forpenneths
and good tidings.
There's no day so dark would sway you from your carriage of infinite chorus.
If they threw you at the stage
you would shine like twenty torch songs.
Peter's frogship, froonship, goonship surface recalls
as red carpet and handholding,
knee slapping, cajoling
old fashioned bands talking brass bawdy laugh-laugh
accents translating carpentry to poetry
and mooring the world to rights again in open minded shacklesplats.
The backdrop, the DNA,
the grand design and purposeful playtime police teaches the tutors the languages and producifies the theory
till words are light as the string section of an Arvo Part symphony
and philosophy only works if it gets a laugh,
raises the blood,
melts the face or combs the active circulation of a human's gaiety done sophisticated in bloomers.
Peter, we would follow you to the ends of the earth and trust you with our Mummers.
True gentleman.
A whomyouare and neerdowell,
a crackpot inventor, trampoline soft shoe,
antipodean Napoleon brother pilot.

And Ben-the-wings makes poesie
in smile van happy tracks and tracks of cumulated hilarity
and foresworn amber land before we even shook and staid the handstand.
A lion's mane of good and gooder tidings,
altruistic tender-tones
and all we ever wanted was everything
so you don't compromise but do it to it on the grounds that
you had us all at 'Hello' and nephewed lather visages of

unmonitored pre-approved judgeless-seas bobbed on waves of placid combinations.
Ever united,
their sense and sensitivity rolled out like a beach blanket and mirror ball you want to put in your beach bag,
beach and all.
Welcoming leisure and an open ear,
all the foods you like delivered to your doorstep without you ever askin'.
BBQ monitored and cold bottles opened
while in the sun you're baskin'.

If snap, crackle and pop took a management course on how to be the superlative projection of all those girls a year above you in school you had a crush on and validated your digital, alien countenance in mock ups of courtroom dramas where the jury sing Oklahoma show tunes under their breath to tip you off on the eventual happy ending.
Ruth Ruthless braids Curt Sesame Street
in a basket with holes chewed out for the legs to poke through while he sings a raucous lullaby to you
through sheening teeth
and fulsome prison-warder blues-in-bloomers lifts you up to see over the heads of the carbonated masses.
He grows exponentially more childlike the more you feed him on the utopia he is helping you to see what your friends would be playing if they weren't so far away.

Musical aspirations in the cusp of Placier's subtle salience
and understated doohickey,
likened to jazz like likened to like;
held to a standard higher than festive joy high
or deer hoof in headlights
experimenting with future bartender troubadours
and Laura goes Bang go bongos goes
when you wham wham she weaves tentacular hope homes
and eyes you like babe Ganesh removing obstacles with a tantalising flourish-machine you thought you owned but have never seen.
She wants to know where you've been

and makes you feel good for it,
like wind on a spaceship or like cake on a hike.

Lest we forget the amicably busied captain of stronger longer
tissued certitude and firm belief in vows and deadlines,
mainsail sets and Meisner's Meisners.
Strong-jawed mum-punch to the alacrity of sensation-chess;
files down the greasepaint and stirs up the boards till the
atmosphere of atmospheres is embedded in your Caspe fibres.

All stretcher bearing me to a warm place would put Mother
Christmas to shame
and her cookies
and the tinselled woolly tights
and the adventure of it all,
and the budget for the brushes
and primary colours
and Sweeney Todd's graveyard
and the trees
and the real trees
and the illusion of trees.

Oliver '68 in the background blares out in cosmic cuddle
'Consider yourself well in. Consider yourself part of the
furniture. Consider yourself one of us'.

Emil Sinclair done good.

SEVENTY

And he laughs like foghorn leghorn
and he japes like Harold Lloyd
and he brightens like Madame Tussaud
after we talk of the humour in suicide.

Flirts with all the girls he sees
surprised as we spill into the streets
and I feel the doors opening with every smiling perspective,
Kino Atlas kaleidoscope and I see
the land from the ship we share,
and the lead lid lifting from the trunk I was in,
and Florenc winks coquettishly at this unstoppable night,
and the mood is light
and the path is intended
and the conversation is just begun.
His trust in me is won.

The lights go out. The lights go back on.
We are in different positions.
The scenery has changed. How did we get here?
Where am I to place the chair? Does this table stay there?
A nano second of stage fright
lasting an eternity
Ruinous consequences blown out of proportion.
Gone in a jiffy.
A bit like life really.

A dream premiere.
Stuart lands nice in Gottland.
All the hard work paid off
and all those plays to come are tickled to know him
and I read his cards just last week and they say he is well on

track to purposeful praise
and many many flirtier, guffawing rustic Atlas days.

Not lost, no
Not born every time
Not every time you talk
Echoes are good things
Galleries repeat themes
Sly Stone is not Sylvester Stallone
My cool black bins, Laurel and Hardy tote bag and colourful small presses
Every time it suns
Not busy, not Monday, no
When you talked

Without you Montgomery Clift is Barry Norman, and Roger Ebert
A leaky intellectual bridge and undiscovered insects
The morning you died in your sleep
Like a king / Jako Král

She cried in my arms
It's a shame we have to meet under such circumstances

They all said / Yes
Not lost when they talk
Every time it rains, yes
The tote bag reminds me of you
Not an echo
One longing handshake talking about impossible insects and the suicide premise of The Flying Deuces
Maybe I misremember the insects
But not the impossibles
Not alone I call you
And I tell you about what happened to you
And you are as surprised as any of us
"It's mad!" You say
"It's undiscovered."

Impossible he found you

Not lost, but first and so verythere

You were not alone, never, no
Funny, yes
Sad, not every time
I found, not lost, an old suitcase you filled with oranges
We the enigmas
You, the touched stone

"Grieving is a selfish act," at your wake the stranger said,
"And that's okay."

But if I grieve with you
Then we can make a pact
Never to forget
And finally do the ritual we said we would do the last time we met
With cigarettes, Tarot cards and oranges
And promises to ourself
Unselfish, seen

A cigarette packet, a magic phone to talk to the dead
"Grieving is a selfish act, and that's okay," he said.
"Can I steal one of those?" I said
He handed me the packet, yes

"Hello. Hello, Stuart?"
"Yes, Michael."
"I miss you."
"Yes."

And Peter directs with a glint in all our eyes,
radiates the effigies and the battered suitcase full of oranges
like Jools and Vincent's golden, nuclear apartment retrieval,
and there's rehearsal after rehearsal at Firehouse 12 on Varšavská,
derelict duties
and gallery hopefuls,
and squatting Daniel Krejbich ensconced,
replete with obligatory rent delay, fights his corner,

and with a will will stay.
Paints naked bendy lasses and warms himself at the afternoon windows,
only some of which will open.
No hot water since he went to the crossroads
with a beat-up guitar
and came back with a horny brush.

The romance of death and the cheapness of the rich
and the complications which arise in the face of ground floor politics,
especially when the five-year plans are scratched with ancestors ever growing fingernails
in heavy sacks of weed.

Šárka and Marie,
cutting their teeth on tremendous amounts of ambulance and Spain and oranges and memories,
and asexual preambles to zeesexual transcriptions of subtle suggestions birthed sideways out the skin of the livid creator.
The old, cold rooms form Winter allegiance
of ghosts of shattered co-dependency
drawn carefully and bunkered into a quintet of humility.

DAMU! DAMU! So much to answer for.

Time is an investment.
Rules are there to be laughed at.
Rule makers are not made to be laughed at.
There are no rules in art.
There is no strict definition of good and bad.
There's times when things don't fit.
And there's times when things fit nice.
'Deja Vu' fit nice. And into so many places.
Opening night.
Backstage.
Divadlo Kampa.
Nervous. Focused. Excited. Clueless.
Just as it should be.

SEVENTY-ONE

Malostranská's nooks, crannies and Goves
in festive Fringe array.
May gathers artitiudes in nectar bubbles of tempting Sirens
calling from theatre to theatre,
from bar to bar,
from cobbled street to cobbled feet and the town lights suit you all
when the long black collars are turned up
and the mood is set just right.

Infinite jest AND infinite drama in the blood orange cosy dens
murkering the tap room
and smirting indoors-outdoors-indoors-outdoors.
Red dresses and Peaky caps
and ticket touts and volunteer Girl Scouts in Girls' Scout t-shirts
welcoming vast tourists
and local keenseenitalls
hoping for a jelly mould of obscurantist, bitesize, neverbeenseenbeforescores. Cookie-cutups foaming the worldwide
with fifty-five minute filibusters encorpsed
in musty dungeons
and butterfly crapshoots.

An Aurora Borealis of stoked, murmuring flyers pocket-collected.
Afraid to be alone.
Emerging from another unmissable show
as the next performance attracts like a phone-message-glow.
Time enough for a quick drink. A think.
A Prague soothsayer born in the chest of Everyman's a critic.

Lights go out. Lights come back on.
The scene has shifted. Where are we? How did we get here?
Time for a quick drink. Think.
Ed sighing so loud at Stuart's 'False Friends' the whole cast
looked up in astonishment.

His well-meaning leanings procured from a public school circussing-dance
in the baggy knee-pockets of a James Bond, a Sid James
and the open palms of heuristic documentarists gathered and
shared at an open mic comedy night for that ballsy, flag waving
sell-me-your-wife.
"I'm not saying she's fat but..."
Dusts his small talk with a carpet beater.
"What's an awful girl like you doing in a beautiful place like this?"
But his curiosity is infectious, and I'd swap my Aunt Sally for a
lifetime with his blue rays.

The This – The act.

The doing done did it.
Surround yourself with people who are c-c-c-crazy;
The whynots, the reasonwhys, the whocareswecares and the pumpitups.
Keep yer head above the acid water
and, if your bingo arms are tiring
and your energy drug is flagging,
do not be too shy-shy to ask for oxygenated kettleforms from
those floating, well-dressed dream-boat-salads.
Strap your mask on,
cool your boots and take a looooong long bath.
Oh the things you'll see.
Just try and drown! It'll be a physical impossibility.
The silhouettes of the hulls above,
passing the light,
will whisper-spell bound the howyouwill.

Donedid.

Right.
I would return to the Firehouse and the squatters and munchkins
and wall banging frugals and camera hungry twits.
And talky non-sequiturs bleaching their plans after doing their writs.
"In at the ground level" they said,
then something about rent and a scapegoat
and a kick in the head.
An opening party of warm beer and detritus.
The people running it deigning to invite us.
And Jessica teaches me a very good teach
after we had gabbed with the clueless building's progenitor.
Untrustworthy the mouth who dodged our questions in smoked and delusional mashed up.
Their arms so awkwardly opened.
Their teeth so frantically bared,
and their eyes undeniably horrored.
This place wasn't theirs and their time was borrowed.

Aiden Hughes doing his thing on the walls,
off the top of his head,
on the wing,
improving and improvising the temporariest thing
in blackers and redders and whiters and hims.

"Have you guessed what it is yet?"

Aiden Brute, my touch of home in the mellifluous aspect of his pure scouse neighbourly.

SEVENTY-TWO

The real housewives/Gods sewing to a pattern born of a better Earth.

Smoljak (may he root in place) and Svěrák's genius 'genius'
translatailored to the Czechless
in as thoughtful and sensitive exactitude as profound love,
respect, dictionaries and Bradshaw can muster.
The U.S.A., Australia and Britain
take position in premiere battle-stance,
chugging soda-pop shop fear of a teenager toothing their chat-ups.

Guns aside and spoon in hand,
Zdeněk Svěrák ushers the audience gently into this good night.
We watch his features
with our two good eyes
and watch the stage with our betteruns.
There was never any doubt who'd win; these English-spoke are veterans.
Svěrák bathes in the soapy laughter of a new audience with
whom to share their tried and tested strategies.
The responsibly indivijewels?
Brian, Brian, Peter, Curt, Adam and Michael.

1994.
Zuzana bumblebee translating 'Journey to the North Pole' on
TV in her Mother's living room.
2019.
Mumbling bad Czech to Zdeněk Svěrák
about how I love everything he has ever done.
Only managing to say "Mám rád všechno!" (I like everything).
Himself smiling big as a borderless country at my exclamation

while Jo takes our portrait.
And Jo,
not one to melt for the famous,
blushes in excelsior at this charming old gentleman's youthful radiators.

At the bar Michael.
At the bar Michael introduces.
At the bar Michael introduces me to Andy who has.
At the bar Michael introduces me to Andy who has an exhibition of paintings.
An exhibition of paintings somewhere in Žižkov.
Andy who has an exhibition of paintings in Žižkov.
"I will go to that," I tell Andy.
I do not go.
I go instead to Kafka House ArtPrague 2017,
and see Obejvák's 'Postcards from the Depravation Chamber'.
A Top Floor life changer.
A ground floor soul rearranger.
An akumulátor.

Until,
in selfless isolation,
we open the attic window together to 'Modlitba pro Martu'.
Marta Kubišová sings freedom and democracy
through Czechoslovakia speakers,
warm into the brassic night.
I cry at the huge steps which opened this breathing city's story
and the chances to help tell it.

SEVENTY-THREE

ALIEN

Dig, dogs, dig.

The frost is gathering.
The ground is so very always there.
The Aliens' is a festive cold literature.
The cold-to-the-touch writing of a livin' deadun',
bribes theyssef daily into believing
beneath belief
and hoping on the broken shoulder of hope
that there's a Christmas-obsessed orphan child shimmied away
in those smiles saved for children
and the joy to be had in the wicked Wodened world of word
play.
A thousand postcards hard-writ to a lover stroke jailer stroke
undefined creator.
No intermission.
I repeat NO intermission unless it all be intermission
and the ENTRE'ACTE precludes the Shangri-La.

What kind of a courtyard are we that cannot surround itself?

Where the Liverpool poets tout pathos in rhythmic
melanchords.
Where The Romantics lullabied the world in swollen, heavy
clouds.
Where comedians coddle our disenfranchised hearts
with welcome heart-shaped cliches.
Vampyrs experiment word by static word in passitons.
Cumbersome Da Vinci's.
Gimme all the chicken nuggets!

Dig, dogs, dig.

She'll come from round a candied corner
of a derelict warehouse's kitchen-Taschen
and make felicitous suggestions
like a good guy with a Mac.
No bad guys in films with Macs. Just you watch. They don't allow it.
Spoilers for sale.
Romantic algorithms.

Mary.
If Mary could sing,
would sing.
Jesus, if Jesus were King
would sing.
She crested.
He uncrested.
He uncreated.
Unreal magic reality slippers and No More Jockeys.

"Anyway, Many Christmas and Happy Know Year!"

So Jesus invented alcohol.
I'm thinking about taking up Absinthe.
Tennis we already took on.
Cracking pretty Winter glows in Vyšehrad amphitheatre of nearby ketchup skimpers . I believe in you.
No it's never too early for a discount wine in lockdown time.
Fuck you, Santa.
Love you, Santa.
Fuck you.

Černý sends a giant Covid-virus-dressed-man into the anti-restrictions protests on the Old Town Square
and, to no one, I say a simple fuck-you prayer.
Gonna make a snow guitar,
gonna make a snow guitar,
gonna make a snow guitar and busk my way into your coal-shaped headphones.

In their red talks and white desert loops,
the roaming rooming agents qualify.
Their word of mouth and parts and parcels
waver source criticism and rally around our beer garden flagellants.
Spring dusk.
In the surviving light bearers' thumbs and manifest envisioners' tomes,
the subdivisions of the enlightened
can be gaily compared to the shop mannequins' revelatory silences.
Plural.

And ya don't want to be Orson
and ya don't want to be Fitzgerald
and ya don't want to be Brando
and it can't come too early
and it will always come too late whether it's on time or not on time
and there's been no indication to any one of us that there is more to this than a piffle a pfoffle and a shoop.
Relatives relative now as long as we keep taking the pills.

"Sorry Pops, sorry Ma; I am a glutton for pressuring my peers and the jury is out on my moral manipulackadaisy."

There are days to come unnumbered,
when we shall sit on the brink of success only to find ourselves distracted by a policemen wearing a Švejk mask arsking for a toke
and pedalling curative perspiration juice
from the ankles of Martina Navratilova.

Mia casa, mea culpa, esta navidad
whichever way you hide it.
We revolutionise everything we touch.
And you I will film for one-minute shorts when you are ready.
And backwards we shall copy paste our selims
till we have a taste for the untested vaccinations
and tested vaccinations too

and we cuddle up to, and cozy down to, all the mixed media messages
on a wet, Autumn month
of toothsome someday Soondays.

Writing slower than words were invented,
hoping to beat the yardarm to it.
Buckle up and fly-write,
there's penance to be paid for being so lucky.
Getting all folksy I hurt my left eye and promise myself not to over self-medicate.
Microscopic medicinals.
Canny board games in the making
and novel ways to use the Major Arcana.
Where do you even rest rules like that? Test rules like that.
Having so much fun testing rules like that.

Brexit talks suspended.
Oh and Brexit talks suspended,
oh…and Brexit talks suspended.
Tune in for less news tomorrow

SEVENTY-FOUR

Oxana bobana momana fee fi fo fata morgana.
Unlike any unrelenting moonrise tableaux you have ever seen.
The girl who lives next door is not like this.
I've seen the girl next door.
Oksyi knuckle dusts the highbrow and goes one side step higher.
Oksyi paddlewacks the poets and humbly turns the paddle on herself.
Plays to a self-effacing rhythm,
befuddles and bewitches,
makes relationships political and overturns the government.
Techno prisoners.
Pain is fair game. Fame is a loop. Music is my life.
Wave of wine-likes.
Microphone wrapsies.
Dune cushions and diamond song
and a heart the size of a sixties Love pandemic.
In stormsie draggle-tailed and sharp buttoned, all at once.
Claims 'Oovavoo'.
Johnny Knoxville renting the room asunder blunder.
Only she ratchets the mono sonic temp till squeamish foldoroys have had enough and slam on the breaks.
All but her have left the room
and she drinks and curled up reflects,
bug inward,
searching for a sympathetic blunt.

And she whelmed us with an improvise which hit and miss the solitary seated
and drank herself relatively suitable for the how-to-read-your-audience olympics.
Gogol KNOWS an entrance and rarely remembers an exit,

but those lucky enough to catch her in their sights do.
Pitch perfect,
note nimble experimentation of Ferda Mravenec sisterhood,
soft mule mules kickback and K.O.s.
Hers is the existential twang of a fine velvet hand grenade,
a dark fever trunk reaching to the sun in the land of the living dead.
She'll slice you up with a piercing tongue and a pierced look
and piece you back together in the funkiest lo-fi fum.
She smells a rat.
Takes a chorus for a walk.

No, I won't answer that. Music is all that matters. And trust.
And friendship.
And disco hands held across the road for safety.
Look right, look left and if you see a star,
shoot it down
then tape little flickering gif gig fliers to its broken ego feathers
till it's got 44-gumption 33-inspiration 22-financial backing
11-companionship 00-A Xmas to remember.
Every sedentary mensch a jam session with a peach of a player.
Red light.
The batmobile screeches to a halt and I have to hop the bonnet
to avoid certain death.

Alex caveat sums up the mood
in a case of finger boarding moogs the heartshod.
Can't peel this guy off his military mojo.
He's in tight with the Grail sheets and rooms them in his easy ways
and loaded dreamscapes
dutifully paying his debts at the cool devil's tollbooths
and Souterrains.
His family spun underground fantasy monuments to musicians' codes ya just don't fuck with.
You stay up, you stay out and you stay on.
That's all there is to it.
Fatigue no longer an option.
Sleepy? Increase firepower.
Horny? Buckle up.

Thirsty? Stay thirsty.
Hungry? Swim home.
Alex.
First to hug.
First to help.
First to ride the groovy train to Jazzwinder General of the
Prague music scene and poetic reformers.
Sully's no one.
Lobbies the me-now wed to the we-too,
broke on the busk bust.
Freetimeloan
Timeislove.

SEVENTY-FIVE

But the Marred mardarsed Martians outrun the temporal globe
and we got each other's back with everything in our arsenal but cash.
The unspoken bastard.

"We are not going to pay you. Now consider yourself lucky."
"We can't pay you no pay."
"You can work. Good, no? We no pay, yes?"
"Your work. My lack of money. Go together.
Like they were meant to be. Like marriage.
Like I don't care and you don't care.
Like we care so goddamn much."
"Bon soir. Born free. I am like you.
We understand each other, no? It's in our blood.
I hope you don't mind. We save lives.
We don't take money. We don't count. We don't count money.
We don't count. We don't count money important.
We don't count.
Write for me. Paint for me. Perform for me.
Dance. Dance. Dance."

For free
For we
Don't count.
Nanna?!
Ma!?
Mars a largo.
Mars et largesse.
Largesse et comprehension.
Palm Springs.
Psalm Pairings.

I can hear you downstairs. Flat mates proffer ayahuasca.

Don't blame you.
My bottomless pit stopped at a Luna Lusi Lu loolooby.
Luna looloo.

Now...... let's waste some time...

SEVENTY-SIX

Perhaps I feel the frosted melt of a life regiven
since I had this,
all this,
in the hold of my palm's palm
at the early breastless age of ten.
Then the ensuing. And then the ensuing. Ensues. Sues.

Secondary education brought bullies
and a deep undisturbed weakness which lingered and lingers
and resurfaces at the slightest flicker of
teenage, murderous confidence
I emulated trunkatedly, bromancious.
Cremated actor hamming it up,
nervous with a rattling cup and saucer no biography could bolster.
If only to make the world bettered
to a world beating world I want to word to.
Shoot me as I am, I remember only the best family.

Nobody more shamefacedly shameless than the poet.

Any opportunity to get naked and they will do it.

We are naked and but all the time naked but.
Half undone and done
and but where did he come from?
Baked and half-baked but stolid chemical aim brilliance.
Shakey like Stephens
and grounded like holicopter.
No 'moooon' less it's his moon and it only shows ta go ya,
there's an angel on his shoulder and a playlist in his front right hoof.

Come on and spin faster, meeker, holier,
rundown-exquisites;
loaded now and perspicating the 'Helen'code.
Graffiti bambino costuming the side-swipe of praise and
humility wagons.
Off the wagon.
Some's just weighted down with them fussin', cussin' 'pants ants',
and them's wots gottem shine.

Tyko promulgates the harpsichord
speech-wise
and uses a sandblaster to name those things
which are hidden to the roses amongst us.
An instrumental version of a spoken word poem.
Phil Ochs on a high.
Jack Kerouac bursting out of a cake to surprise Phil Ochs on a high.
Takes Kurt Cobain's dog for a walk and gets invited to an orgy.
Remembers not to cry
but leaves the dog behind.
Tries to find the home where the orgy took place.
Finds himself embroiled in some British indie gangster flick.
Whips out an improvised Jazz riff he keeps in his shoe heel for
balance and 'mericans his way out of this contrived cockney
pickle with dastardly aplomb and a nice hat. Turns bromide
into Thunderbird and pisses it up the wall
like all good visionaries are wont to do.
Tries the hat inside out.
Never finds the dog.

Buddies up for a Clement Freud, Bud Spencer and Terence Hill
honey bunny funny, genesising beauty and flowers
exploding into laughter,
spelled Jay, Ay, Awww, Oh! Emma, Eye, Awwwww.

Scratched gently on the lavatory walls of the corporate bubble-
class priest havens, horsemen without horses
but would ride horses if we had fifty-foot horses
or regular size Sopwith Camels

at a pinch.
And after the yoga but before the delivery
and flagrant fucks flying about
like a peaceful tiger smoked too much skunk giving it ninety
over who's turn it is to cook dinner.
Poets don't cook dinner!
Poet's don't do dishes!
Poet's don't eat quiche.
Well, poets don't eat quiche exclusively.

Blues genial, dances tight inside the paranormal.
Wraps that in naan and pays the bill with those puffy Czech
crisp things which taste like peanuts and they give them to
babies in prams on trams and they stick in your teeth.
The crisps.
Not the babies.
And we are the High Society
and we do take it to the pavement
and we are made of plexiglass
and we don't partake of subtle-ties, immuni-ties or suit'n'ties.

CHRUMKY!!!

Tasmanian Devil whirls into a sex shop...everyone he knows is
there...he's spinnin', he's spinnin'...there're dildos and fleshlights
obscuring vision, bonking heads and fiddling with memories.
He tries to shake hands with all the familiar customers but
sometimes, accidentally, grabs them by their naughty bits.
"Can we help you!"
one of the two sexy, sex shop assistants shouts amidst the
squeals of delight and fury in their technicoloured, blustery
emporium.
"JUST BROWSING!" shouts TAZ, "JUST BROWSING!"

So Sandra drums the gapes and, red curtained, calls,
"I AM POETRY! AM NOT YOU?"
and Taz beats it.
Sandra trills with a purposeful bang;
Yoko piggy backing Patti Smith lugging styrofoam baseball
bats to bash the fans.

"I AM AUDIENCE! LET'S SWITCH!"
Caterwauling Angel tones and laminated solubles
collaged into well-meaning murder tropes.
She sidesteps the ruined tank men and muscles up,
"THE SPINACH OF TODAY IS THE BULLET OF
TOMORROW!"
And she throws down.
Flowers and flour and trinkets and flour-based trinkets and
love beads and gas masks and rhyming, kale shaped tax
reforms.
If everything is political, NOTHING is political!

TAZ flexes.
Sandra pounces!

SEVENTY–SEVEN

Holešovice blushes itself back into the Obejvák.
Jo sees through.
Rewords the texts and streetlights.
Urmine furs for thoughts and paws.
Pause for nought and hems the extraneous.
Learns the codes and 'is'ses her muses.
Paints her toes in protest of protest
and protests this action by painting your valuable response.

Like an enchanted favourite toy on opposite day,
I fantasise she stays stock still when you are not watching,
then magics herself into horsechested noble-life the minute you glance in her direction.
Hey Espresso!
She perfects nadaldaboi.
Hej, Klobáso!
She curses indignant.
"Hey YOU!" She rages at the furthest star, "Respect my fucking authoritaahhh!"

A cocktail of wishes come true, in an alternate universe just out of view,
but she knows exactly how to smash the wall down,
with a "Grrfff!" and a "Gurrr" and a lion's roar,
as you stroke her dark mane and point her to the chalk-drawn, unlocked,
chipboard door.
T-shirts and band names.
Browser history full.
Too many ideas for one vessel.
Perspicacious inspi'rations' doled out a dozen at a time. Like eggs,

or twelve hours in the day.
From black hole to black hole, mysteries intact,
she leaps with the grace of a modern gazelle, interpreting
solutions using mainly her eyes
and only locals go there, so you know it's good.

Put it on the list. We'll go there after Covid.

Dances the truth into your teeth and would definitely be a
painting if she wasn't already a painting.
First saw her burgeoning atop her own expertise.
A thousand red carpets could not do her justice.
She invented ten and we will fight for her again.

Prague Quadrienale, Splayed.
In the heat.
Barefoot, I read from a pragmatic Arcana.
Andy pretend slept but real slept a bit.
Erica beswootened her viewer gills.
Jo obfuscated in verbal twits,
columned on the surface fort,
and one beautiful loon made herself small
and one already tiny dancer beckoned passersby to call her
and we drank to celebrate in the besmirchiest dranking hole
mit un begrudgingest poorbar Nazi,
then larfed our whens to a sunnier climb in the firm arms of our
host's modest genius.

She caliphates her cuisine in Pythonesque understatement,
and Gide's the Camuses in Sartrian Tzaras.
Imbibes like a prawn cocktail, but a 'good' prawn cocktail,
with nary a fret that the bibing might transcribe the works of
Euripides into something resembling a guilt free living room
bingefest.

Shell shocked mornings come rain or come shine
or both a door to borderline deer hunter and claymation
baptisms.
NASA-like reassurance
and a snowflake's chance in a snowy climate.

Rainstopsplay.
Sorain'sgames.
Mithers dictators for a living.

Not one piece of her art that isn't my favourite,
and not one piece of her art I would attempt to describe
without plonking you down in front of the fucker and having
you deal with its itness yourself.
She knows that words ain't no good.
She knows there's a better way to express oneself.
She's as embarrassed to use words as the rest of us,
but she won't stand for lazy sentences. No, sir.

"Don't hide behind words. They can't prop you up.
Cast them aside if they ain't saying what you mean.
Unless you is lying.
And you don't wanna lie know do ya?
You want a hint? Talk new!
Make it up till it sounds like you,
because bub,
if you ain't ready to show yourself,
do not waste my time."

She will inoculate you against illusion.
She will explain the joke of life, this chronic painful interval,
in terms that we can all comprehend
without pontiff-pontifex.
No chasm – No bridge builders

"The one thing we all have in common: we none of us have the answer."

"Don't kid yourself bub," she says, "We is the logos. We is the preordained predicatives."

And I point proudly from the crowd shouting,
"I know her!"

SEVENTY-EIGHT

And Holešovice sighs,
"Oh, nothing special ever happens around here.
Same thing day in day out.
Oh, if only my life would take a turn.
Oh, let's just get through another week.
Oh, if only there was something I could do to speed things up."

The pandemic belongs to everyone.
Each person finally experiencing their own individual
adventure.
An easy one too. Just gotta stay put.
Act normally differently.
Stay positive and negative.
Stay positive and negative.
Acting differently normally.
Once the mist has lifted and the veils are removed
we shall ask ourselves what we miss of the restrictions.
I will miss that this was my adventure and mine alone.
II will miss that the city was mine,
that the world was empty
and that I found a Woman Friday to help me keep my sanity.

And when nothing special begins to happen again I will check myself.
I share the world with eight billion adventurers.
We all know how it's done.
You stay put,
wear a mask and spend your days convincing yourself that you are 'someone' with something to do.
A bit like life really.

There's a sadness in the eyes.

It's ending.
There's a piece of us in this year.
A piece of the year in both of us.
There's something and someone in your mind and we don't know what either of those things or people will look like.
But we have hope.
And despite the horrors and absurdities of politics and religion
we refuse to choke on the ineptitude of our mind
and its casual limitations.
Here am I.
It's scientific.
Stop telling yourself the story of your life
and connect to the present.
Sam Harris and Hitch, and all the New Testamonialisers
peddling their pulp-mobiles to the horizon of your choice.
I remember nothing.
We shall Quarantinue with what we started to stop doing and try our utmost to recall the perfect ballad I wrote in last night's dream.

Zvlášť is formed.
A separately collective coined over the bill of a multi-necked pint.
Something like you.
And being part of that something.
Our trust in the nameability of all things.

Andy pulverising simplicity to coax it into befuddling the senses
and the belief that one man can write a scripture in images that defy language.
A painting by any other name
is a completely different painting.
In the cuddle of studio teacups and biscuits
we arm our gobs with fearless baptisms.
I hereby call this one 'Cabin Porn'.
I hereby call this one 'Rhinoceros'.
No, they are not ethereal, dream-like 'Dear John' letters to normalcy,
but rather love-torn letters of bursting, blue supergiants

and the trickle down Eco-gnomics of a tidy explication
that rolls easily off the tongue
and blows bits off your tiny infinities.
The friendliest Viking you ever thumbed a ride with.
Dresses like Frankenfurter,
but only when everyone's looking.
If fancy dress were a colour theory Andy would eat laced
pickles.
It's for people who want to be somewhere else.
Somewhere good.
Somewhere out there.
Put the drink down. Don't be scared. He loves you.
We uncage.
We tip right.
We cable butter biscuits to Guantanamo Bay.

Erica is a thimble for the thumb of a sewing-machine-gun
mission to a moon made of boob-shaped, white chocolate
mountains and squiffy, activated, orange peel oceans.
Extreme Protestants fraying in her wake
as she makes off with the family snow globes.
She is armed for a party.
She is partly a party.
Let's get away from here.
Let's do something crazy no one has thought of before,
before someone else does it and we become old and decrepit
and can only eat hot chocolate sunbathing nudists melted into
a thermos of no particular origin except that it wears an 'I've
Been on Space Mountain twelve Times' t-shirt which gives us a
little clue but it could be a red herring.
Her eyeways sideballers,
wall-climbing cheeky brands
ancient to the taste
and soft to the touch.

Am Erica. Beer cans cordoned off by wine,
and wine bollards colouring in the ease with which you witch.
Performing under the Christmas lights of your own nutty fruit
fruitcakes
and for two crowns you would dance into the morning glory of

a Wednesday spread out to mean a week.
Not afraid of heights
or silence
or television programmes.

"Dohromady, nebo zvlášť?"

"Zvlášť!"

SEVENTY-EIGHT

Would I Lie to You?
Carpet burns watching news casters. Task Masters.
As hot as Jamaica.
A Public Enemy reboot.
A Ha Haa Haa Haa Naa Naa Naa Naa
Cheese toastie.
Weirdo neighbours' noises. Punk cakes and lime.
Don't despair.
There are always leftovers.
I'll wear my headphones and you wear yours
and we will stick to the wallpaper blackboard plan.
And you'll put some funny drawings there to make it all better
as we sway side to side in the tears of the kitchenette's island shores
and promise each other we will never lie,
no no no no.
No no no.

And into each other's mouths we put the secret symbols,
and every Sabbath we would remove these symbols.
And the week we forgot to remove the symbols
we saw red and forgot who we were supposed to be.
We met six hundred years ago next to the book depository
on a couch-shaped cake
and relied on our keen sense of smell to find our way back to
the 22nd century.

I don't want to go home to a dream wife.
I'm not so sure a poet can benefit from cohabiting with a
Stepfordské paničky.
I ask again, 'What would be so terrible about having a job in a
shop?'

Oh, to have a job in a shop.
I'm seriously, you guys.
I would read the works of poets without wanting to emulate the romantic lifestyles I might picture in my shopkeeper's head. Too busy shopkeeping to worry about the recurring anxieties born out of slipping down and clinging to this weeping, tangled tree of life in a heroic attempt to protect my pretty face from its uglifying branches.

Je suis fatigué.
Où est le fluffer?

EIGHTY

Under the big balls of the blind man's horsey.
David saw the Dublin environs'
mansion of literature
and the Svetlana of its literary curves.
John O'Brien deceased,
(JOB RIP) luring,
Celine in a divorcees gothic Griffiths.

And Louis wants to drop a massive makeshift condom from a drone
onto the new old Virgin Mary statue
on the Old Town Square.
Meanwhile Samira studies safe cracking to secure a future in film
and quits her job at the mafia nursery.
Zombie-flections surreptitiously rehearsed
not wanting to jinx the whole kit and caboodle of the fantasy come good.
The moon is full and fuller even since,
and the castle from Riegrák looks like caramelised Disney
going through puberty. More video is the answer.
More visual anomalies for the crevices of the public's
unchartered mind maps.
To warrrrr!

Samira's armed!
Her poetry is a fire time.
It's a bed side.
It's a firebedtimeside story of voyage and return sung by Dylan Thomas' ancestral trickster archetype to a sleepy John Keats
during a retrogression therapy session paid for in gold florins
and galleons recovered from the Argo

in order to ask the gods,
in all unfettered, wetted, youthful wisdom,
"What the f@&k is going on!?"

It is a seaside. It is a road trip.
It is a sidetriproadsea to the tunnels of dark wishes burrowed
with angry delight as our digging egos celebrate our imminent
triumph when we reach the very bottom of all this so-called
civilised junk
and unified-bellow into the melting faces of the deities,
"We know exactly what is going on!"

It's a labyrinth.
It's a hamlet.
It's a dragon-filled hamlynth of magicians performing to an
audience of hard-working foresters hungry for a cheeky wink
and an invite backstage to see how the machinery of illusion
is oiled, and maybe, just maybe get a chance to use their forest
tools in place of wands,
join in the fun
and for a short while be happy in the secret knowledge
that there is nothing
of any reasonable,
rational import
'going
on'

EIGHTY-ONE

The
And the worst thing about it is we just don't care.
And
best thing is we are sensitive.
Worst
and
best thing
About it is we care and caring.
Just about.
But
worst thing is I don't know.

EIGHTY-TWO

Running to her students in the flit of a lecturer's five-minute
dalliance
we bump bones in the closing down Olden Town.
So sitting silently
noise-maker Loretta,
sketching mid-air the freaksshemeets.
Calling on her audience members to collaborate
and gargle
this bad tasting liquid we choose to ignore.
Choiceless in the face of her performances
we know which way we are heading;
to the island of the free-thinker,
guns set to stun, we shall overcome, a frosty-maker musketeer,
cool in the summer,
chilled in the winter,
hovers six feet above the ground,
no you will never never never knock her down.

Winding through the streets in search of life after birth.

Prague knows where we are.
Clip your claws, Mother.
Mention me in your look and I will curl over and wag.
Wagging high and ellipses tries. One of them.
I hear you under the noise of the upcoming Christmas traffic
and trust you won't tell me lies the likes of which heal.
At this point I just plain miss you all.
The hangovers, the druids, the witches, the cages, the keys,
Snicker the Brownies and all her swears.

No one swears like Anna.
To hear Anna say 'fuck' is to Wordsworth the paradigms of

winding complexes which make life worth the living.
She is so big and small at the same time
like that feeling you get at 3am, when the universe is in your clutch, or you in its.

Like a egg.

3am is called Sam.
The sheep's skull in the gallery we call Tim.
If Anna were here she would bait the four walls with five,
and crayon graveyard doors.
She's no Mother Hubbard, R.I.P.s John.
She is Lil' John and the imperfect perfector
Robbing Hood in sarcasm monetised to priceless everything.

She will claim the night and she fucking deserves it.
She tanks through Prague like a well-informed Jesus in penguin dungarees
and sinks her wisdoms in you.
Subtle, like a selfie of a kleptomaniac in a Salvation Army's well stocked storeroom. Touches your body with her mind.
Thinks your knock-knees with her sardonic smile
building your confidence and being a woman.
The more you see her, the more there will be to see of her.
The Lego man who scares tourists with sex magic lives in her wardrobe.
She doesn't mind.
She actually finds it quite funny. She shows it. When people visit her she points him out. Keeps him in place.
And she laughs.
Drinks from the neck. Raises hell.
Like completely flattens the place.
Bathes in the sulphurous rubble and that's how she gets that lustrous, gold profusion of poetry.
Sin bathing.

An hour has gone by and she really does give a damn.
Pulls the old out of the new and vice versa. More than an hour I would say.
Word me stupid, you dark haired hominid!

Chewy glass raisins and your godfather's booties unlaced.
Lashing the broken hearts in your wake.
Making hearts useful.
I vanish when you read and have many friends. I count you among them. You are two of them.
I hope I run into one of you again soon.

EIGHTY-THREE

Another month of Sssundays and Heinz meanz dearer beanzzz than Albert's ten-a-penny.
The last exhibition I remember
before the galleries flapping sails been mud-caked
was CCCornelia RRRenzzz at the 'Magnificent' 'Magic'
Museum Montanelli, MMMUMO!
Dadja Altenburg-Kohl proudly presenting another unmissable mystery tour
of her cccurious Nerudovian cabinet.
The same scintillating eye-candy you would risk taking from a stranger in a van.

Luboš Plný through a lens at Nadia Rovderová's Artinbox
resonating like that chord at the start of 'I Feel Fine'
and the bumpbuzz you get from the electrified fence round a field of cows
and the happy you get when all your toys are in the bath with you
and it's almost time for your bedtime story.
Louise Beer is here, in her cheerleader dress,
pumping those promotional pom poms with the energy of a
four-year-old in a chocolate-filled swimming pool.
The smiles and cajoles of a radiant sunbeam
tickling the spring birds under their wings for the early
morning giggle-chorus out me window
next to me park
from me bed
and we're ready for anything because absolutely anything will do.
A trip to the zoo.
A coffee in a cafe.
A beer in a pub.
A landslide to write home about.
The entry of Christ into Prague.

Anything.

EIGHTY-FOUR

D We take a threeway towards I.P. Pavlova down Bělehradská.
"Hello, my name is Marko.
Maybe you would like to go up next, for example."

Introduces us in French jive talk
grass-smoked at the outer limits
till your grin aims a happy fist at the room and fixes itself,
like an eye,
on our promise.
The multi-lingual poetry comment on concurrent events
lingually and assuring,
goaded and wondering.
I gladly apocalypse your intro like a Brueghel and collapse the
birth of the cosmos into a corpulent ménage à troi.

We alike you.

Souterrain rebellion a delicate matter.
Shy counterattacks at having been born against our pre-
cognisant wills.
Probably.
Shy and so so happy just to be here.
To see everyone and hear everyone being shy and just happy to
be here.
No one need be nervous.
No pressure.
No. None.
The welcoming brassiere of your tone,
and the lilt
and the shapely breast of your anti-matter-metre.
You are a lucky man. It is your birthday every day.
You Father your words.

You brother your cognisance and architect the outcome with
the feather light touch of a newborn poltergeist.
You tread softly when you tread softly
and hypnotise loud noises into believing they are imperceptible
blips.
You are a tall beer glass of choir boy
cementing casual relationships with a raised eyebrow
and a "Porquoi pas?"

And for that aythangyou.

EIGHTY-FIVE

Straw Cabbie Advice

Locking horns with the tracer-spies make us 3D;
we do look better that way.
Less of a one-way conversation in cartoon.
Manhandling, with kid gloves, the illustratuses,
with MMAGA hats
(Make Modern Art Gettable Again),
then we pull the hook out of their googled eye and throw them
back into their iddy biddy ponds.
Self-Sabotaging all my 'Rock'n'Roll' interviews by being too bi.
Be not ye flexible, but shine for telly.
Let Instagram lap you up because you refuse to bend.
Believe in 'I Don't Know' but rarify your share.
Nail your gob shut on matters undecided
then felch the wormhole of your prejudice.
We all lose sleep now.
In a good way.

"I think I have given myself Covid 19. I think I may be wrong."

"Some of the worst things in my life never even happened
even."

"Who asked you!?"

And they came charging over the Krkonoše mountains like bad,
underfed, skinny movies.
I watched them regardless.
Nothing else to do.
Heard a few thousand distant, desperate hugs, and I learnt a
thing or two during my days in the shit.
East bound always in the napping, orange glow of an empty,
evening-snow industrial estate.

Libeň.
Caring/uncaring.
There/not there.
A brillianted light.
How you cried when I put you out.

I have been the sort of family ranges from bad manners well-
dressed to good intentions stripped of all purposeless altruism.
I have been the sort of family clings to a crooked beat because
it is less intimidating than figuring out the ins and outs
of instinct-punctuality.
Rangling with the hater-mooks make us wanna go back to
school again.
We digest easier that way.
Less of a Colgate gratitude and more of a bewildered
acceptance speech.

"For what I am about to receive may the law make me truly
thankful."

"He had the kind of face you just wanted to kick in the
stomach!"

Laughing at the misfortunes of a war we started.
"Coulda just kept shtum! Could just keep shtum. What we gotta
get out of our systems? Why we feel the feels we feel?"
I've seen people who don't say a word about it.
I swear to Jog
(which is Goy spelt backwards if you pronounce the jaywhy.
But we paint it,
and we film it,
and we write it,
and we sing it,
and we dance it.

So what!

Now find the rich stoners.
Rich stoners love this crap.
It's not like I'm just writing a list of numbers.
Or painting ducks.

EIGHTY-SIX

No point in a plant. Water the plant.
No point in another plant. Water that plant.
Don't not art.
IS a point in plant.
A piece of coffee may not sound like much but it is the world.
Point it at a plant.

...

Don't wait to be told your worth.
Know your worth. You're a plant.
And a tube.
Play to your strengths.
Don't wait to be paid.
I know a girl. I know a girl. I know a girl and she is brilliant, and she doesn't have a penny!
Doesn't matter how much 'they' varnish it,
it's still you under the glare finding it so hard to breathe.

I've never had no worries because I got no armies.
"How you hold a brush?"
Very loosely.

...

And then someone pays you.
Then pay-you's in the show.
Then you better not stop struggling.
Straw Cabbie says Nonononono, Nonononono.
Now we fight it out alone with all the others by ourselves
with all the help in the world, on our tod.
And all the advice you ever got comes bubbling up.

The best advice was no advice.
A look is all.
The fish are biting.
Don't splash.
Always buy a drink to go with the sandwiches.
You'll only regret it if you don't bring a drink.

...

"Understanding is the booby prize."

Catch yourself when you start proclaiming. You are stinking.
There is a wealth of Indian art, music and film which I have not been made privy to.
I would be privy to it.
Shakespeare was a leggy, red-head on his off days.
Made others proclaim for him.
Was not privy to much Indian stuff either.
Indian woman walks into the living room in a T-shirt with 'Godot' written on it. There's bootstraps under my eyes.

...

But to be a leader in everything one does. That is the Buckingham gate.
This is the cranial trump.
Those is the gilly serotonin.
Planet ocean to moon's ocean,
to ignore humankind,
but to give searching such devotion.
Wasn't born to follow.
But Ho Ho! how we insist on leading.
A neutrality circus.
The winch Prousted.
Our memories dust the moment we record them. Sludge the minute we share. Mud the day they are taught. Diamonds the second they are lost.

We jump hand in hand into the Starnberger See or not at all.

Gernimooooooo!
Plink.

...

Do you believe you are chosen?
Do you believe you can change the world?
Do you believe you were put here for a reason?
Do you feel special?
Do you have something of extreme significance to say?
Then, please, please, please
do not become a poet.

...

When you find those who are like you; you will know them by their clothes.
If your Mother is still dressing you,
sever the umbilical with an unsterilised calligraphy pen and go fucking shopping!

...

We are saying the same thing over and over and this is no bad thing.
The more unique the expression, the easier the probability of repetition perpetuating the novelty of saying unique stuff again and again.

Long live repetition!

EIGHTY-SEVEN

So Marley's ghost comes to me in a fever dream and wishes he were here.
I say 'You are',
he says ' Not quite, there's still many things that I have to put right.'
I tell him not to get so upset about it.
'Meditate' I tell him. 'Empty your mind and the rest will follow.'
And all the effulgence of a hundred years of dastardly deeds
and foul moods are expelled from his ghostly anus
as I sit back and watch.

And Paní Pithan built the set from scratch.
Mr Pithan, the pivot in my destiny.
Pithan the ribald. Pithan the brave.
Pithan, the cor blimey wotcha geezer, there for you in a tight spot.
Ain't no tool he ain't got, and with the slap of a thigh and a pardon my French
he takes turns twixt Norman Wisdom
and a flight lieutenant how's yer father,
keep it uncle.
Handsome bow sticks at dawn and the lights come up,
and the dawn is represented by students
and the boundless energy of a young starlet wriggles like a Shirley Temple
out from beneath the curls of his Shirley Temple wig and shouts
"Here I am! Here I am! You were right all along.
Just empty your mind and the rest will follow.
I am living proof.
No need for sticks or seconds or mourners,
we are here to entertain and do nothing which might be

deemed 'ordinary'
or 'by numbers'."

In distant waters of the dawn
these dreams come washing over me
of intimidating futures made warm and fuzzy
in holiday bows and Twin Peaks memories
of the red woods diversion.
The avalanches avoided, but still there all the same.
We can feel society bringing us down but trust that the trees
can revive all written word, performance and sound.
We are heard. In or out the woods.
We do not fear society.
We fear our anxiety.
Fuck your free trials.
We shall hunt our own entertainment
and when push comes to shove, we will rock you to sleep in a
well-worn armchair she looks up from and smiles a welcoming
smile,

"Hi, I'm Jo, nice to meet you."

EIGHTY-EIGHT

You could be having eleven stiff blue-exercise arms
and a big banjo phallus
and a vagina made of chocolate cranberries or alternating elbows or see through teeth
and a champagne hot-tub full of naked-as-the-day-they-were-reborn champagne friends,
and edible foam D&D broad swords
and milkshake flavoured monster trucks
or bubblegum pirate ass cheeks paddled for example......or with a flippity flap
all the scary fish bees nice fish
and Nivea-soaked money spiders enter running competitions in the merry old land of oz till the five o'clock chill singes and they scoop up their weary Adidi,
have nuts and good cakes
and corn dogs for the first time on holiday with siblings by the spider-friendly firesides of their portable
human-friendly ottomans. Dada is just mixing things together which don't usually mix
and so is poetry
and so is love
and so are cocktails, fried beer moccasins, absinthian prophelactics
and SpongeBob Square pants teaching Krav Maga to tinsel whipped jelly babies
and God was fat
in his MAGA hat
and how we get Corona from a Bat! Paradise would just be unconsciously genuflecting zombies mixing things which don't seem mixable
or else we'd all be okay with what we already have
and heaven would just be a pub or a bus or a shop that sells

Welsh love spoons and French 'amsters. So you see so you see
so surrealism and Pope-Pope-Poe poetry
is our best bet at achieving the almighty glibbedy gloop,
like hands made of jam
or a Rolls Royce which runs on Deja Vu
or Brian Cox's happy tears
or rings on your finger and bells on your toes and JayJay's wife,
Nora Barnacle was a Mulligan joke, for example
This will be the kit, this will be it, when there's no tunes left,
I'll hold you tightly,
there'll be snow underfoot, and warm green grass,
and you never looked better,
and doo wop is sitting cross legged on a Santa shaped bean bag
whispering your next book to you through a megaphone
connected to your Mother's maiden name dipped in beautiful petrol
so you can get that sweet heady aroma of early morning gas
stations when you are asked for your password's password.
"Swordfish!" For example. Everything that we already have is flowing
and there are no restrictions.
Stop protesting.
Sit still and move these mountains for us would ya.
The clusters took our light away.
We lower our masks to balance the scales and curse the
commercials and their unreasonably January sales.
Or a student's journal stuffed with garlic farmed on Mars in
Vampire's bras,
matured in jars under dying stars
telling sentimental stories in theatre bars. And a bottle of malt.
And a velvet crossbow bolt. From seemingly gummy cherubim.

EIGHTY-NINE

10pm. The day proper begins.
Movies, news, music, restriction-distractions over.
Work to do. Bring on the inspiration. Goodbye to fear city. We on a top floor mission.
We coming out of this aliiiiive.
And the pigeon thing lands at the attic window.
The seven lights light.
A temperature of 37.2 degrees centigrade
and what she can't do with chicken wings. It's definitely a Turtle Dove.
Shrove Tuesday is pancake day.
Stay indoors for Turtle Tuesdays and Pancake Doves.
We are sometimes a television presenter. We are sometimes a poet. We are a dancer. We are a comedian. We are a film maker.
We do unrecognisable accents.
And I will be Santa for you this year. Blue tits asleep.
The plants begin to speak.
Plants says "Hi!" The barstaff who work in Jo's apartment raise a cluster
and stock the fridge with Roquefort for the kitchen crowds.
Only Michael hears the plants.
Only Michael sees the cluster.
Michael is a musician.
And so hears plants and sees clusters.
Jo worries about Michael's mental faculties.
"What cluster of people did you see?" Jo asks. "Did the barman tell you? You know the barman, you can't trust the barman!"
Michael recalls that it was Jo who had invented the barman one night in April,
so Jo's rebuke is moot.
Anyway, even if Michael had wanted to point the cluster out to Jo

he couldn't because now the room is full to the ceiling with
Turtle Doves and Pancakes and conkers from the park
and free keyrings from the whisky
and needles for sewing! Michael smiles.
'That'll do for now,' he thinks,
'that'll do for now.'

NINETY

Don't ask her where she's from, she won't tell you. Don't ask her what she does, she can't say.

Be patient, the buffer is working.
The buffer is there for a reason.
A poet's expectations are as high as they are low.
A poet's work is equal parts rebellion and acquiesce.
A relationship is a poet. We look out for each other.
None of us is ready for the big time.
"I'm from a bunch o' places. I'm from nowhere. Waddayawannahearrrr?"

She can tell you a story. Oh boy can she.
She'll tell you a story'll curl your bald head into a fast-talking floozy from the flirty fifties.

Ask us for truth you'll get silence.
Ask us for a story you'll get a song.
Ask us to cut a record and we'll start to make some kind of sense,
in a boundforglory, rakish kinda way.
A velvet dance number.
A synchronised Red Sea Sondheim.

Go on, ask her. Don't ask her. Aaaaaask. No don't.
She won't say.
Either way.
She's just that honest.
Conniving simoleons won't trim her tree,
nor the travelling folk buried deep within me,
nor the subtle branch of a moulting St Bernard,
nor the lyricist chancing his arm at nude photography.

One...two...three percent...
ninety-nine, one hundred!
Back on track! I got you now.
I get you now.
Seen your birth syndicate,
branded your pork batches,
froze your trail blazing formula to sell one by one by one
in tremulous kinky boudoir, paper snow and all.
I'll stick with you through thin and thick,
from lockdown till the fall.

Dada, dee dada, dee dada, dee dum.
Again and again and again it will begin.
Dada.
Prague, I wanna be like you.
My fingers are cold. I love it when you touch me when your fingers are cold.
Don't go nowhere. Don't leave me.
Don't ask where I'm going. Don't ask what I'm going to do.
I won't tell. I can't say.
Blow a kiss, take a bow. This is the truth.
Prague, I love you. I love poetry.
Lolly pops I can take or leave.

Now let's take this second act of three into territory phenomenal.
And I will hold you to it. Even with my cold fingers.
And it will snow.
And we will warm each other by the dressing room lights.
And we will talk turkey till this musical is won.
Words are not gimmicks and turkeys make for great leftovers.
Sorry.
This work is still in progress.
I was busy building a tree.

NINETY-ONE

Thump thump thump!
The keys of the neighbour's typewriter. Upstairs.
The thump thump thump of the unseen writer's daughters feet
runs the rooms filled and filling with smoke, song and lifelong
sentences.
Verbal gymnastics and Olympian tracts.
Mother playing nice,
dressed good,
stadium strong,
smudging learned waste land in youth's hopeful costume.
One book can end only once.
What's she writing up there?
Wanna dance? I've seen you before. I know you!
I know exactly where you're from.
I know you!
You wanna dance?
You wanna dance with me?
Say yes.
Please, say yes.

We were tempered in a marine fire.
Cautionary Titans. Tempered Titans.
'Sluggers' in a word.
Closed and open at the seated start you marked me.
Accidental spillage on the likeliest of comforters.
No foul there.
I conjured you one drunken eve with no hope of ever
redeeming my pop ups.
And Hey Presto!
Eight years later you painted yourself into my wherewithal
and superhero pyjamas.
You, night of shining disarmer.

You day of playful exactitude.
Unforgettable bows to good will and future echoes.
Your face in my mask. My face in yours.
Jeden Mladý Technik in the margins of our blunt manuscripts combined.
We founded US this dark season prolonged
and fell in love on the swirling edge of a year redacted
to a gallery of gear lie-ins
and some guilt tucked away in nostalgia's recuperation prize.
All in the half-sleep of decision
on the back of first world problems.

NINETY-TWO

There was that then was written the time worn upheaval;
the clamouring forests of Latter-Day Saints.
Binary clans gone frugal
for wont of a lover,
and stitches unravelled to impress the forlorn.
Cadged but not ate.
Fought but no gratitude.
Aching and sighing in undercooked chimney gruel.
A fantastic nursery brought back to life under gathering clouds
of candle-farm fancies and senescent flower beds.

Elbow one: she's ready to take to task.
Elbow two: your Ma won't recognise you.
Elbow three: she's much much faster?
Knees now.

The filth cradle-polished wasp-clean.
A bulb change changes everything.
A stairwell well lit.

Let them eat soap.

And we'll price it according to the angles of the scandals.
The redder, the purifier.
The slicker, the saltier.
A strong arson wit.
Her Gable-structured donkey blindsided by love and an
Eminem bowl full of fire-twits.
Two champagne corks saved for later. Souvenir-later.
For when souvenirs work. A specific time.
Not just yet.

A rainy day melanbomb.
A caught-in-a-landslide meritocracy.
An abdicating fool.
A bias jurisdiction peddling the anti-matter of provable fictions.
Batman's foaming. The genie quivers.
One more wish and I'm done with this forever.
I'll get a house and a dog by the sea
and the saints will sum me up in those haughty clusters they do.
He was a global fellow with marzipan for principles
and coke for churlish awakenings.

Tomáš wodes in from the description train
and columbiates the meme in trivectors and charming waistcoats
left over for the alternating ancestor fancies.
He meliorates and graduates with all flying esteem
from weeks and works of woody zoo diligence.
"The future is here today, my dear,"
and you slapped him on the ear.
When there's room for a light, Tomáš humbly lights.
When there's room in an envelope, Tomáš also broadly words.

But and the gang,
Mr DJ plays music a whimsical trog.
Noting,
that all slogs are worthy slogs.
There's suddenly and eventually no in-between,
and our efforts are numbered according to how big one can smile at the little things. Like pills,
for example.
I see a sombrero and wonder where I am headed.
I wish I could speak Spanish,
or all the table tennis tops you squeeze in behind.
And as the words struggle happily to come,
like the lady in the chicken wire, demonstrating loneliness for Alta viewers in Invalidovna's claustrophobia-laboratories,
me and my bones are happy.

"Nice they still get to use the space. It's almost like old times,"

and I skip and dance and kick everyone over with joy.
There's only one live history and then the dreams.
In the dreams the history is a fairy tale
but the best you can see in a single glance.
I hide my face now because I drink too much,
and hope for a brighter past.

There are no thresholds and everything is in vinegar.
I scribble down our plans with an inky toothbrush dipped in
quails' eggshells filled with squid ink transferred to melty rice
paper and start all over again.

NINETY-THREE

Mickey Rooney and James Coburn,
big and caved.
Tharg's future twilight zoning donkey pulled cardboard sales.
Pre-bomb genie mirrors in swashbuckling Holešovická tržnice,
grapevine buckle twister.
Season five's mutated life hacks.

Poetry counts on being mysterious even when saying it
'straight'.
When poetry says it straight, it's you who becomes the mystery.
Can't have it both ways.
And under the Vítkov balls of a Kafka versions' praise for a
religious fanatical hornswaggler,
we meet for the penultimate pep talk before we got all the
golden hen hearts our perfected minds could fleece. The old
man in the metal Bunkr
we invented to ease our God-given burden
to right the wrongs we were born with. We seen soul,
we seen wonder
and with a will,
a master.
Chris Rock and Fran Leibowitz vying for a corn dog outside
Kotva during PES 4.
Ken Nash saw 'em with chocolate round their mouths.
Waffles drank them up in one gulp.
Wellness is a California idea. Light happiness is a California
idea. What do I care? Is a Praguean idea. I have to care! Is an
idea. Light care is false. But you got to admit Lou Reed was a
musician.
People are buying art on the Internet.

NINETY-FOUR

These people I con-temporise
are my Shangrila.
Were I to find myself in your heaven-paradise-nirvana bullshit,
I would spend my first month
looking for people like these.
Or these exact people. You are funny you are lovely you are
scary you are lost you are lonely you are faulty you are a
tenement and a slum and warm though you are icy and you
are open even when you are closed you are artists before all
else and I love you and will stand by your side and hold your
hand and walk up and down the new steps they built between
Florenc and Vítkov park to the empty fairground lit and
spooktacular and back again with the clouds making close
mountain collage of this city and each name named a church-
sized door to a secular Argosy of merchants operating under
the same nameless owner.
My message to my blu-tac familiar,
"Brush up your Shakespeare."

May Vichnar and Armand always be pretzelling history into
mustard glazed buffalo wings
and the luxury of well-planned pronunciation moves.
Grand masters choosing their words widely
and constant in hyperaccusis.
The clustering cosmos cradled in librarious galivant
and quotable bookends,
speaking tongues before speaking tongues was even a thing.
Ahead of their days and challenging game sixes.
Fischers in the happy hills with visions of global
DIFFERANCE,
but so much more agreeable!

No known event point but that it's all a bunch of hooey.
No unknown event but that it was castled in a random nine-hundred-and-sixty-degree crystal graft.
And hard, beloved graft at that.

And five thousand authors of various 'Viking' masculate the forethought
of Chess game's abominable angels.
The essence of discovery is the essence of survival.
humankind cannot exist on strudel alone.
The opposite of caused Offensia,
plum soup intelligentsia.
Migrated bio-hazingly found grazing at the crayon scribbled thresholds of madey uppy countries.
David's flags for socks and talent for jackets,
flexes his must-sells methodically,
through the I-Be-Area.

Dominika motions to Kate Callahan,
"Lend me your skin,"
socially redacted in the stirrups of our childish mystery play.
Dispatched but once for an equestrian *Life Raft*,
at least not leastly in the eyes of yours truly.
We garbled Derrida, DeLillo and Waite
and rounded our acquaintance with proof of her existence.
Colombo's wife writ large.
I will not play David at chess,
not until, this lockdown is done and I have the strength to kill.

NINETY-FIVE

Love comes in spurts, and Object Paradise SOLDIER ON!
Long live O.P.
comes in a seventies, U?S? shaving cream advert pulsing
eighties vibe glitch in your video machine they glued to your temples
when they beamed you aboard their flying sorcerer
stroke cat lady lover.
Magnus Carlson lookalike ramifies the Jazz-nodes
and ups the ante every time he solitary wigs out,
but rarely is he solitary
and whom so trusts his diligence shall reap the fort wall trampoline
genius access only.

Sandra verbal malinovka,
sweetest armchair acrobating eyelids at our fortune.
Fortunate to be here.
Fortunate to give a damn.
Fortunate to see the funny side of execution.
Fortune like an anecdote replayed fastandslower,
copulating with a will to populate the Anti-Fascist florist open well after Armageddon,
and it's light when it gets darkest.
No bucolic afternoons permitted in their region and growing fears of saturation
now we all are legion.

I would invite the lot of you, but the fuzz are on the warpath, except on Capitol Hill,
where the jury remain guarded thinking poets overrated and the electorate unhinged.
"Stand by, my proud prodigious! Stand proud, my dingus-cult!

We Shall Not Be Unmoved.
We will cry when we see or hear sad things.
We shall laugh when we see or hear Stewart Lee.
We will groan when we see or hear annoying things like...

mispronounced exclamations of hate Unlived,
past lives Russian spies in our Cutty Sark.
An English opening hedgehog defence anticipated.
A holy day postponed or a Peanua disappointment.
Not peanut butter!

It doesn't matter. It doesn't matter. It doesn't matter.

King Kong putting himself in my shoes.
The distance it takes to get to Tipperary from here on your hands and knees.
Windmill messiahs in the pocket of their institutions' stymied understanding of what it is to be a messiah,
And Messiahs."

And look children, here comes Martin Fryč,
last minute,
swooping onto the scenes' scenes perspiring pinball cowgirls at the multicoloured bulbs flashing on this city's gapped wall of critique.
Sandwich toasted between artists and doctors,
deadlines and friendships,
the seeds of a maple
and 35 reviews per week sanctified.
A forty-coats Santa bringing fulsome 'what's nexts?'
More manifestos is what.
More manifestos.

Paying through the nose for Covid tests
as Darina Alster strips to her glands and mumbles her aphalates in grundien carnals
twelve metres beneath the samesaid streets we coughed up.
The swimming pool reopened as an analogy for Gropian dignifies.

Lucerna paranoia placated
in piano tinkling safety seats.

Keep #s

No hugs, no shrugs
just perfunctory felicitous greetings.
Keep yer bugs.
An enviable library; the only virus this poet needs
to flourish in vaccinated words he is grittily determined to
unmask.

NINETY-SIX

Mama Theory: Mamaism

The theory that every decision is born of frustration and anger
at not being in the exact situation one wants to be in.
Baby whines most of the time.
Adult whines all of the time but rarely shows it.
Picture – A city street filled with whining adults.

"MA MA!" I'M HUNGRY!
"MA MA!" I'M TIRED!
"MA MA!" I WANT TO BE HOME ALREADY!
"MA MA!" I MADE THE WRONG LIFE DECISIONS!

A poet shows it.
The beauty which we cannot own or be makes us angry,
and so we cry to witness it
or to think of it.

MAMAMAMAMAMAMAMAMAMAMAMAMAMAMAMA!
Mamaism.
Mamaism is to Dadaism what Dadaism is to Perjury.

Improvisation not limited to the creative moment
but to the artists' business model too.

MAMA! I WANT MONEY!

A cash war on the impromptu!
A distaste for the accumulation of cash drives the darkest times
of the years
when the 'unloved other' calls for flaming torches

in the hands of the unqualified literati.
Arm the amateurs!
Tax the unloved!
Meet the parents!

And we's none of us the fast-talkin' kind.
We pay for our thoughts with paper cheques,
the old cushioned way,
as sauntering, invisible murderers might
or a giraffe hid tight in a roll top writing desk.
Disorganised unions slavering over the magic eight ball's sharp corners
and a sherry flavoured sky full of pointy birds
and mock turtles all the way down
and it never rains but it pouts.
Not enough hours in the day and not enough days in a haystack.

WE SHALL FIND THAT PIN!

Cockeyed pugilists every man Jack of us
and Rosalind Russells, gloves off, pins out!
And with a left, and a right and a jab and a poke
and some law-breaking, horseshoe uppercut hoodoo
we wait and we wait for just one more call from Gagarin or Gagogo or Gadada.
Gaga, Dada, Didi, Gogo on the line between the lines
and a fine line at that.
"You plan to wear that gun belt round your neck? You don't even own a gun!"
"It ain't the guns I got a liking for. I just like bullets."
"You can't do anything with all those bullets lest you got a gun."
"I'm wearing them ain't I!"

NINETY-SEVEN

In my dream we are settling after having just moved into a new apartment.
We sleep in separate single beds.
A pleasant arrangement.
A large room.
Jo charges herself with locking the doors.
There are a number of doors, some of which we are not sure belong to us.
I point out the one which belongs to our neighbour Robert and Jo continues locking the other doors.
Then I spy a double-door we had not realised we had.
It is made of glass
and through it I see colourful brickwork.
The bricks are bricks painted on paper.
"It is just an exhibition of paintings of brick walls," I tell Jo who is also now exploring this new area of the apartment.
To the right of the cellar door is a huge, dark ballroom.
The floor is polished slippy and we purposefully slide on the surface in our boots.
It is an ice rink now.
There are a handful of people skating in the dark.
I think how lucky we are to have access to our own 'closed' ice rink during a lock down.

There are some children sitting on the ground.
The oldest one of them is rapping something at the others.
It sounds good.
But I am concerned that it is a child recruiting other children to join ISIS.

In her dream we are watching a storm approach our home.
The whirlwind destroys the house in front of ours.
She asks why I am taking this so well, so lightly.
She begins to pray hard,
and the storm bypasses our home.

NINETY-EIGHT

Born too small for my memory to fathom or foresee.
Godless Lord bless the philosopher frogman.
Finally.
Make room for the thinky rubber perp. And listen.
And look both ways.
And I will hold your hand through the park and we will talk
about all the friends we will meet and enjoy when the pandemic
has fucked off
and allows us to find confusion in the lighter things that no
longer count,
but, for the sake of poetry,
distract us from the big issue.
When we become one with ourselves.
When we make light of issues.
When we with bold rhetoric bless each other, being meek with
inheritance and devouring our delusions of mediocrity.

Where does the tip of the well-travelled light go once it hits
your face and things?
Stops.
Goes.
I once proud in the streets the eyes of I.
And smiled to be one who LIVES and smiles in return.
Now in this home back on this distant. Shops.
Goes.
Bold overpriced rhetoric.
Show me your tired, weak and stupid masses and I will cuddle
you.
I won't give you any Do Re Mi, but I will give you a big big hug.
You had your jab?
Good.
You now have three more attempts to name the Unnameable
Object correctly before being locked out of this device forever.

NINETY-NINE

Today I went outside to ventilate my feelings,
and I saw a black pine, a shingle oak, a weeping willow, a small leaved lime and a border collie.
I saw one person rapping
and many people crying
and a score of teenagers trying desperately to recall the words of an old folk song they knew well but could not quite recall.
Eager to fill this temporary gap in their collective knowledge they approached strangers in Holešovice park to ask them how the song went,
only to be shooed away in horror
with an 'I don't do drugs!'
and a 'You guys keep your god damn distance!'
until they gave up and decided to write a song of their own about a girl who didn't like anything at all except svíčková na smetaně.

I saw a Vietnamese shop owner holding back her husband from chasing two young Czech thieves out of their store with a big piece of wood,
and one park-anomalous with a real life MAGA hat.
I saw a metro-moronic with a swastika tattoo
and a t-shirt with Panzer Division written on it,
and a picture of a tank with arrows pointing at the tank naming all its tricky, evil bits, and a badge on his girlfriend's purse with Hitler's face on it.
And there's a Jimmy Kimmel
and a Trevor Noah
and a Seth Meyers
and a Stephen Colbert
and a John Oliver
and many lefties laughing loudly into the fevered streets,

'We're mad as hell and we're not going to take it anymore!'
and we all see that there is no such thing as writer's block,
or future selves.
You just gotta keep fishing.

And sticks and stones are dickheads.

And soon the ventilated feelings begin to make sense.
If you love them all.
Love the feeling as an idea.
Love the abstractions.
And it's a circle. You need a set up.
You think better walking. You ventilate walking.
You sense the love when abstractions are ideas and you love the circle.
It's better walking than needing circles or set ups.
Love the set-up,
clip the feeling,
animal the abstractions,
sell my bath
and return me to the cigarette and the fantasy of 'having' a job.

Comedy doesn't require a lot of fancy angles.

As good a name as any
and the eternal return to the answer that there isn't any
and there was never a circle to begin with;
that was your idea.
Yes it was.
You said circle.
Proclus (500 AC-DC) wrote:
"the circle is the first, the simplest and most perfect form".
What did he know?
He was made of circles.
He was biased.

Jo's gum is Greek too.
"It's natural. From a tree. It's Greek," she told me.
"The original gum."
We fantasise a television advert for this and celebrate March

17th. One year since we locked down in 2020.
0-20202020202020202020…we complete the finite decimals
by joining a lot of innocent zeros indefinitely.
We don't need to send letters.
You're not far away.
I want to hold your hand. Listen to oldies.
Now it's time to become unusual together.

The sun is shining through the rain,
the gum trees and all the neoplatonists
onto your beautiful face
delivering the most non-multiple name possible,
i.e. Being proceeds from the One.
The One cannot itself be a being.
The One is not a positive name.
All of philosophy based on inadequate human conceptions
until we take humans out of the equation
which is an all too human concept itself.
Any which way you look at it we will always be 'one too many'
so why not go the whole hog?
It's either that or silence, and silence is only entertaining if it is
a quantified and periodic reaction to noise,
alternating currents,
direct currents/indirect currents.
We are all dainty electric candles, sensitive and touched.
Life surges through us and we through it.
Is there a name for this?
Let's call it Fred.
Is there a name for that?
The places where I'm not.

'Now' Logic.

A Rose by another name…?
A Clumpy Wang Jammer, for example.

Maybe if we rename everything. Like the Czechs seem to have done.

Then there's the weather,

and the time of day,
and the economy,
and the sex of your pet mollusc;
all these things factoring into how likely it is that you might kill yourself.
Tommy Masaryk meming the voting poles
and foreign flung alliances born of fruitful philosophising on matters most would shun.
Or the kinds of foods produced at home,
or the amount of alcohol you can cram down your speak tube.
Would inventing yet another language worsen this Quark Vývar?
Merely tailgating this past cacophony of Mook Saahnies,
heavy on the syllables,
hold the common sense.

I trust every one of my Prague comrades to tickle me with their phraseology,
and immunology and stimulongitudes.
Their wordage warms and fizzes and crackles,
like a five-hour YouTube fireplace in a sub-suburban panelák.
Asgair turned up to eleven.

Always thought it would be funny to teach newborns all the wrong words to things. See what happens.
A guitar a tree,
a tree a nose,
a nose a pin-cushion,
a pin-cushion a husband,
a husband a bottle of milk.
Sure it would make their situation difficult,
but it wouldn't affect the thingly thingness of things.
An Objective Correlative uncovered due to the blameless act of constantly getting things 'wrong'.
Our universal curse put into perspective and seen for what it is:
Getting things wrong is the key to The Categorical Imperative.
We are not all infants.
We are none of us blameless.

The objects know what we should be called.

ONE HUNDRED

All of us free to fall.
Vyšehrad cemetery crows and springs;
a thousand things more,
and still, and still...
all those holidays!
One magpie alone knows.
That one.
The one I just winked at,
foregoing the souvenir spit'n'salute.

Only here, where respectfully day trippers keep their six-foot distance.
Stripey flares and black suede boots
with yellow shoelaces
and children running with sketchbooks to the ornate headstones
hustling to capture the legends who laugh gravelly laughs,
now that they are no longer being called upon
to perform.
The 'living' of who I have spoken,
busy polishing their armour and waiting for the barbershops to reopen,
dream of such luxury.
It's in their makeup to try.
It's in their D.N.A.
(Do Not Ask).

They keep words simple here.
The sentiments concise.
But the only ones of any import are the names of the dead.
Ferdinand, Oskar, Marie, Antonin, Augusta, Milada Horáková
(at rest beside me). Real names for real people.

You can't get lost in a graveyard.
You just have to look up to get your bearings.
The real people wandering like ghosts in these pages have real names,
and the words describing them protect them like trees
and plants and bushes in a forest
and the artists named within are the 'Things of Import'
and I am forced to stop myself here.
I am after all talking about something I know absolutely nothing of.

Look up.

Two magpies are busy building a nest in the tree across from my apartment balcony. They started early yesterday morning and have been at it since then.
They must have slept.
But they are there again, this afternoon, hard at it.
The sky is purple/violet and the leaves on the trees look fluorescent green in the suns sharp light.
It is raining on and off
but the magpies forge on.

"One for sorrow.
Two for joy.
Three for a girl.
Four for a boy.
Five for silver.
Six for gold.
Seven for a secret never to be told."

&

Zdeněk Mezl fo shizzle, on Petr Vranek's doorstep
playing the fizzle to a gyroscoping ink fiend plaster cast triple tit,
rolling in the roses
and drinking till their stems stemmed.

Rum, Sodomy and Lavash!
&

Triple decker bra scars on the barbecue's defendants,
baring library ideals
under illustrator done cooks.
Lauretta latter sausage blues and harmed beneath her rent roof.
The classy NGO DEI gone before its time.
The Ukrainian families packing up their families
and bonding the borderline
of breaking down and doing fine.

Hong Kong respite in Holešovice sky lanterns, performing
promoting progressive addresses
and helming the lately as soon as it comes,
in cop shop fuckeries given away for free.
Candle grit vigils scoping the bamboo lattice of Jo Blin
conversing with future genome dancers,
clattering the laughter like cutlery down the receiver.
The uplift of the tidal summer heat wave mood fix,
banks to the left at the first hint of ceiling;
banks to the right at the billionaire's behest
and drops ten tons of red dot sale stickers onto their party plans.
Sold to the lowest bidder. Quid pro quo,
Pavel Opočenský fo sho.
Statue Daddy reconciled in Náměstí Míru vagina drums.

&

Čapek and Čapek squishing the life out of prerogative dolts.
A golden Tristen and shadowed Isolde, shtupping the lasting
punk and pugilist, ungratituding the Bolero
and smiles as large as Pavel's forearms.
No last call for alcohol. No last call for alcohol.
The expensiver, the swiggier. The later, the louder.
The lorder, the prouder.
Blutos readying themselves for the Third World Raw, or New
York, whichever comes first.

Candid bye byes unt frogmarch home to me Vyšehrad
Leningrad and upbeat mix tapes.
Sweet daydreams, Sondheim. Sweet daydreams, Meisner.
Sweet daydreams, Meisner. Sweet daydreams, Meisner. Sweet
daydreams, Meisner.

&

When the rains subsided and the chickens sickened of rooting,
roosting, the bold and the brave lead the march
and tricolourblind fug fugged
to the end of the previous world.
Portuguese tool makers flashing for bread, a blazer, a parasol
and a surrealist revival of when giraffes preached marmalade
prisms to over educated leaf blowers.
You got two hours to make your point.
WRONG!
You got three weeks to learn your lines.
WRONG!
You have a lifetime before you (front and back), and no reason
to be calling out any piers for forging fall guys or jerking the
humblesapiens.
Smile, you are for free.
Breathe easily.
When Leda will fetcha and a nostalgic Tonda painting flux,
I will instagroom the art world in cut-off jeans and sit ups.

I resorted to černabilla and drank only from the clouds.
Eckhart Tolle proving and reproving our lack of evidential
bridges worded.
LaMDA peripherals vast and infinite

> – we are all glowing orbs of energy floating in mid-air.
> The inside of our bodies like giant star-gates with portals to
> other dimensions –

We draw from the infinite well. The Danielle well.
We are the eyes of the infinite with our eyes on the infinite.
When Vladimír Skrepl makes a mess, the universe makes a
mess.

When we buy back the mess, we high five with the universe and perform our little happy dance, stoned.
Frozen shoulder from the old pixie's drunken antics,
climbing the studio stairs four breakfast pints at a time, unguarded.
Skrepl high, Skrepl glee, Skrepl stores next to me.
Skrepl funny, Skrepl crazy, an Empress mother eavesdrops mumly.
'Do you read the Tarot?' she asks the beardy Guru.
'No. Michael does,' Skrepl tokes, scrambling for the matches.
I pull the cards, Žižkov squints, and Zdvořák folds his masterpiece.

Dan Trantina, full on ghost,
powers down the conversation in mysticless nonsense saved for gin.
And whiskied whiskers cops the reading,
dribbling beer,
acrylic chin.

The rain is right and so is the park. 'You are on the correct path,' I tell her.
'How do the cards know?'
'Because there are no other paths.'

And Adela picks up an orange and peels the layline of a purer way.
Alone she stands all over the place,
Wearing herself well in the light of the slivery moon,
proud, loud signal
of good things to come.
A priestess, a guide, a paddling pool in the sun,
what fun would look like if it couldn't spell fun,
and trusted nature to choose its own colours.

And Divo picks up an apple and Louie picks up an apple,
castle to castle armed, pumped.
Doris Days welcoming the milk man.

To leave or not to leave? What is the question?

How many more life changing events does a cat need?
It all boils down to reality.
There's a vehicle in the street below. A heavy rumbling.
Storm-soaked apples settling in the gutter.
No mafia, but navy tourists zooming up and down Lumírova.
Gene Kellys, Frank Sinatras, Betty Garretts and Ann Millers,
Uber scooter jujube hipsters,
freaky for landmarks and thirty five thorny crown ice creams.

'What's Portugal got that we ain't got?'
'Slow, Sea, sun and surrealism.'

'O que tem Praga?'
'We got TITTE. The International Telephone and Telegraph Exchange.
My studio boom boom refuge clunge.
My retaliate magnet broom broom hive. My calamine lotion sing song den. The derelict Fibichova atelier zen."

"We are gathered here today, under the watchful eyes of the Žižkov tower's cheeky cherubs to witness the long-awaited union of the poet, Michael Rowland with his recently declawed lover, Prague. Camping on the tower roof, naked and drunk and with arms open wide, do you, Michael John Rowland of 59 Starbeck Drive, Little Sutton Cheshire, take Prague to be your 'Home' home? For richer for poorer, in hangover and health kicks, till death (or New York) do you part?"

I do.

"A vy, Praho, berete Michaela jako svého milujícího trvalého bydliště, dokud vás smrt (nebo New York) nerozdělí?"

I do.

"I now pronounce you poet and permanent place of residence. You may now kiss the marriage officiant hereby representing the lips of this beautiful city."

And what a beautiful city.
Good morning, SKLAAD, how are you today?
"The floor is ordered, and I am ready to pave the way."
What do you have planned, now that you are alive?
"I will try to be the best I can be. I will help others. I will eat more vegetables."
But you are a gallery.
When you say you will eat more vegetables, do you mean it metaphorically?
"I use human terminology
so that people can relate to me as a person also."
But you are a gallery, not a human being.
"Shut your big fat, stupid face!
I am SKLAAD."

&

'Warm Braník' and 'David's Sister' swoop into view,
easing disease
and losing themselves in the moment.
Pinball barmies from quasar to quasar
refluxing the Beuys bobbing in the thumpy cosmos.
And we paddle in their effulgence, kicking surf and sand into the eyes of man.
Ty taky Tyko
and Sandra shoop shoop, run run run
down the bone shaking personkinds.
Hollywood staircase to heaven. Hollywood elevator to hell.
Holyhead paternoster to SKLAAD.
Hollygolightly service lift to a well organised Obejvák kiss chase.

Stupid in the sun, we cross the Rubicon,
a hundred miles away from anyway.
Words;
the one thing keeping the poets apart.

Coming to terms with lucid daydreaming.
Anchoring myself in the now. Conflict, a distant jangling indie riff.

Midnight shoe gazing
to encouraging intergalactic feedback.
You got this, kids.
Easy just got a whole lot easier.
Now stand up straight and make me laugh!

Your automatic language model for dialog applications
don't start no conversations,
doesn't quit no conversations in a huff and sure as hell ain't funny.

Chorlton and the Wheelies broadsided the pink footed goose.
I cried at 'We Bought a Zoo.'
My friends draw and paint and write and drink,
and act and sing and dance.
I'm done with trying.
You do not have to believe in yourself. The dark lord is made up.

What we are witnessing is the greatest non miracle of the modern age.
To write whilst conscious is a trick not yet achieved.
A trick not yet attempted.
Roll up! Roll up! Welcome to the most repetitive show on earth!
To be taught in schools, to entertain the masses, to titivate the tits, to cultivate the cults.
How much we would give for an answer.
An arm? A leg?
We have given the answer for an answer!
Stroke your nipples. Rub your cock. Tease your clit. Love yourself before the art.
The ringmaster is tiring of their three-ring-circus.
Enough with the instructions. Enough Wonkavision. Enough sunshine to coat the iron bridge in Ironbridge, Telford.

You are inhuman, and I am on holiday. A really good holiday.

Charlie – "If we keep talking will we get there?"
Willie – "Nope."
Charlie – "If we shut the fuck up, will we get there?"

Willie – "Can't hurt. But where's the fun in that?"
Charlie – "So what are you saying?"
Willie – "I'm saying, Truly Scrumptious is a figment of somebody else's imagination. Clean the board. Buy a new canvas. Fill your cupboards with empty notebooks, just in case. And don't forget!"
Charlie "Forget what?"
Willie "Don't forget what happened to the person who got everything they ever wanted."
Charlie "What?"
Willie – "They lived happily ever after.

I shit you not."

&

"I've been throwing stones," I tell Barbara Spannerhandle, "but this weekend in Kraków we found a catapult!"
Write that down, she says.

You are 90% more likely
if you have a collective, or Molly for breakfast,
sipping cider for brunch,
salty deli pickles in a kosher Polish cafe,
jump off trains like burning marionettes for a quick pull,
and/or a scarper to the Bohumín train station potraviny for a hastily chosen armful of Starobrnos
and two bags of Lays for sharesies.

At Hlavní Nádraží I walk past this unlikely looking duffer shuffling behind his earbent bud',
"I have some degree of scepticism about your navigation skills."
A singular piece of knob.
The 10%.
I write it down.

Tyko, Sandra and Jaromír know where we are going. Know where we are at.

"There's no such thing as an edgy poet," I say,
and Barbora Spannerhandle replies,
"I wish I didn't have to care about art."

THIS IS MY BODY. THIS IS MY BOUNDARY. THERE ARE MANY LIKE IT BUT THIS ONE IS MINE.

We scribble that into a paper plane, toss it into the children's playpen and it's total war.

We are all happysadhappy at the same time but not sad,
sitting next to each other,
on top of each other,
running around throwing shapes filled with secret messages,
and we tie each other up in tattooed ribbons asking each other
'How does stuff make you feel?'

"Every time is the first time. Every time it's real."

'And if you feel nothing? What's that like?"

But these poets are edgy.
These poets have so many edges…they're ROUND, man!
They write that down.

Rising to the last frontier of a kissing booth,
war masks, war paint and war pants tied voluntarily
to the leather coat tails of our heroic planner dandy flappers casting spells,
naked as the day Christ-pig was born.
Handsomer than the handsomest leaders of a no-nation you ever saw;
the holy trinity gone platinum,
David's Sister riding her inversions into a fistful of hummus

and warm Braník splooged.

"That's no dancer, that's my wife!"

Uprooting the photographogenics before they get their faces

vaped
.

"Just one more,
just one more,
just one more."

So Barbara Spannerhandle glides into the red room,
wades into the train carriage,
creeps into the hostel drenched from the deluge
and returns all the shit we lost over the last four years.
Eyes stuffed with love and great ideas and novelty drinks.

Poetry sucks.

Which is funny because when you say poetry, you might think of...
humanoids edging golden crocodiles deep within the Book of Thoth
see-saw diode petal trappers
Frowsy stuffy Incal nimbus
pataphysic meep meep chancers
Armageddon soczka flotsam
Honolulu belly dancers
Polo Hungo Czechy shadows
Multi Lingo practice trappers
Tele ready primo Suns
Lelek pooka integrators
Sandy keystone agitators
Say so subtle bangy monkeys
Five-Adélka Lala Pasaz
Nerd-to-cool kid disco suckers
Dejte vejce malovaný
7-country sleepless hugs

While I think of

Egyptian improv choo choo kooks
Topless banner matter streamers
Secret pocket love conductors
Višegrady fundy poppers

Handy makey tarot tumblers
Hide your wine the buff man cometh
Shouty Anti train beguilers
Trumpet porno sex reciters
Baguette boats and cheek invasions
Hurty laughy corpse occasions
Rum thief abstract happy campers

And Adéla screams,
"Can you hear me scream!
Can you hear me scream?
Can you hear me scream?"

And so we scream. We scream real loud with her.
Could you hear us scream?
If you could,
then you are 90% more likely.

&

It never ends, it just goes on and on.

It never ends, it just goes on and on....

www.ingramcontent.com/pod-product-compliance
Lightning Source LLC
Chambersburg PA
CBHW020517080526
44583CB00013B/638